COOKING FOR ONE

COOKING FOR ONE

Elinor Parker

SIXTH REVISED EDITION

1817

HARPER & ROW, PUBLISHERS, NEW YORK

*Cambridge, Philadelphia, San Francisco,
London, Mexico City, São Paulo, Sydney*

Designer: Helene Berinsky

Library of Congress Cataloging in Publication Data

Parker, Elinor Milnor, 1906-
   Cooking for one.

   Includes index.
   1. Cookery. 2. Menus. I. Title.
TX652.P3 1984 641.5'61 83-48119
ISBN 0-06-015232-X

84 85 86 87 88 10 9 8 7 6 5 4 3 2 1

CONTENTS

5

COOKING FOR ONE

1

WHY COOK FOR ONE?

THE PURPOSE of this book is to help you who live alone and who like to cook but who are baffled by recipes which are usually geared to families of four or six; even cookbooks for brides are planned for two. The solitary would-be cooks are also bored by what seems to be a limited number of possible menus; roasts, of course, are absurd, many vegetables are so large that they will last for days if consumed in single portions, and the majority of packaged foods come in quantities which are impracticable except for family use. No one likes to waste good food by throwing away leftovers, but no one wants to eat the same meal several times in succession. These recipes and menus are planned to show that cooking for one can be both interesting and economical. Although it is possible to buy a whole meal, precooked and then frozen, this seems a poor substitute for home cooking. Frozen main-course or side dishes are comparatively expensive and although tasty are always exactly the same and apt to get monotonous. Also, if fried food, they are generally heavily breaded with little actual food, or if sauced, with a small proportion of food to sauce.

Once you have mastered some simple dishes and the basic cooking methods, be imaginative and branch out. Try new combinations, different seasonings. Read the excellent food columns in the newspapers and try adapting the recipes for several people to your own use. Keep notes of your successes—or failures!—and you will soon have your personal supplement to this book.

Why cook for one? Why not? Save money and eat better!

HOME COOKING PREFERRED

The book is also planned particularly for busy working people who have little time or inclination for elaborate preparations in the kitchen and even less time for marketing. These same people have discovered that it is much more restful and relaxing to eat in the peace and quiet of one's own home than in a restaurant, even if one does the cooking; the wise ones have also discovered that it is far more economical and can be much less monotonous. With the time element in mind, nearly every meal or single dish suggested here can be completed in less than an hour and many of them in a very short time. If a pressure cooker is available, it will shorten the cooking time of many things even more and it will also save precious vitamins.

MARKETING WITH A PLAN

Probably the most difficult aspect of single housekeeping is buying food in small enough quantities, knowing what will keep and how to keep it. Meat is the hardest problem and the small cuts are limited; certainly no one wants a steady diet of chops. However, when entertaining you can choose for your main course something ordinarily denied to you by sheer bulk, such as a roast, something that will give you interesting and different leftovers for your next solitary meal; the same rule can apply to the larger vegetables. All the suggestions here are for foods that can be bought in small quantities; if they stretch to two meals, further suggestions are included for a different way of using them up. Buying tables preface the chapters where they will be helpful, and there is a list of storage rules included with other suggestions in the next chapter on the kitchen in general. Naturally the question of price will determine many of your choices, and you will have to watch the markets and decide for yourself which foods are essential and which are extravagant. Certain foods are seasonal in many parts of the country and there is one safe rule for buying them—wait until they are in season locally, because they are then most plentiful, most flavorful, and most inexpensive. Also, do not let yourself be led astray by bargains in large-size packaged or canned foods which can spoil before they are used up—buy the size that is most convenient for you, your appetite, and your storage space. This procedure will pay off in the long run.

Supermarket packaging, which always seems to be for two servings or more, may be frustrating. Vegetables and fruit can be refrigerated for several days and even this may not be necessary —acorn squash and grapefruit, for instance, will keep on a cool windowsill. Meat, either raw or cooked, must be refrigerated but it can also be frozen (see p. 25).

USE THE HEAD TO
SAVE THE FEET

Much time and effort can be saved with a little thought, and I strongly recommend that you plan both your marketing and your meals ahead of time. Sit down for five minutes one or two evenings a week and plan the menus *in writing* for the next several days. Check with the cookbook what ingredients you will need —especially if you are going to try something new—and make the marketing list for the next day's expedition. A trip to the delicatessen is likely to be expensive in spite of its usefulness in an emergency. Marketing by telephone is a lazy way out and can also be expensive; by going shopping in person you can take advantage of the day's special sales and avoid the more costly items. You can also learn of new products and get ideas for future meals, and if substitutions are necessary they can be made more easily with everything in front of you.

I also commend a plan of *not* rushing into the kitchen as soon as you get back from work. Take it easy for at least half an hour and don't think about cooking unless you want to start something in the oven, such as a baked potato. It is a great help to change one's working clothes for something fresh and comfortable; then sit down in an easy chair with your favorite news program or a crossword puzzle.

Plan a meal that has only one dish on which you want to concentrate. Remember it saves steps to have the whole meal ready at one time and brought to the table in covered dishes. Jumping up and down to wait on yourself defeats the whole idea of a restful meal and is unnecessary if you think ahead. Save future time and effort by cooking something for the following day —specific directions for this will be given later. Save fuel by using the oven—which is the most wasteful unit—for more than one thing at a time.

A GOOD FIGURE AND
A LOW BUDGET

So much information about nutrition is published nowadays that it needs little mention here. The "basic four" is as easy a rule as any to remember.

- the meat group: all meats, variety meats, poultry, eggs, fish, shellfish, legumes, nuts; two or more servings per day
- all vegetables and fruits; one serving of citrus fruit or tomatoes and three others per day
- the milk group: includes cheese, ice cream, and yogurt; some milk (in any form) every day
- the bread-cereal group: whole grain, rich or restored—check labels; four or more servings per day

Other foods not specified include flours, sugars, butter, margarine, other fats. Try to include some vegetable oil among the fats used.

Cooking for one can produce as well-balanced meals as cooking for any larger number, and nutritional essentials need not suffer.

Appetites can vary considerably, depending on one's sex, age, physique, and activity. *Average* servings have been indicated throughout, but you may have to adjust to your own requirements.

Remember also the following three rules of variety when planning:

- Of *flavor*—for instance, if you start with pea soup, do not serve peas or a similar vegetable with the main course.

- Of *color*—a meal of fillet of sole, macaroni, and cauliflower might taste good but would not appeal to the eye and thus stimulate the appetite.
- Of *pattern*—the conventional dinner of soup, main course, and dessert is not a law which must be obeyed.

EASY DOES IT

Breakfast is your own affair and is not touched on in this book, but it is wise to remember the importance of starting the day right nutritionally. Follow your own inclinations as to what to eat, and allow enough time to eat it slowly. Don't overdo it in either direction—your morning's work will suffer equally from too much or too little breakfast. And if you are dieting, all the books will tell you how important it is to allot some of your calories to breakfast and cut down at some other time.

Lunch for many live-aloners is eaten away from home in the course of the day's work. The menus in this book are for simple dinners, which for most of you is the important meal of the day. In choosing a well-balanced diet, let your selection for lunch work in with what you have planned for dinner. Perhaps you like a large lunch and a light supper; there are suggestions here for suppers of that kind. You may come home so tired that the soufflé you had planned so blithely the night before seems like a tremendous undertaking and all you want is to have a tray in bed with a minimum of effort; some emergency meals like this one are included. Although planned as evening meals, any of them can of course be used as luncheons when wanted. Some suggestions for brown baggers or lunch at home are included in Chapter 4.

All the recipes are planned to save time and trouble in the preparation, to save washing a lot of kitchen utensils, and to save stocking ingredients which will be used seldom or which will not keep. Besides this primer for single cookery, it would be wise to have on your kitchen shelf for reference a good basic and complete cookbook. Any single recipe here can be multiplied, but why not branch out and try some others that are not practicable for yourself alone? Some specific ideas for dinners, buffets, and cocktail parties are contained in the last chapter, "Entertaining Singlehanded."

One further hint. Since you are your own waitress or waiter as well as your own cook, do treat yourself to a little style. It is just as easy to set a place at a table—or on a tray—with attractive mats, china, and glass. It's so good for the morale too. Such pretty things can still be bought fairly cheaply, so no one can plead economy as an excuse for laziness. Your cooking, however superlative, can be even more appetizing if well served. A glass of wine makes a pleasant addition; many excellent table wines, red, white, and rosé, are produced in the United States and are amazingly inexpensive.

2

---⊗---

KITCHEN NOTES

Individual preferences about kitchen utensils and gadgets are as varied as individual lifestyles. Therefore I am not going to give an extensive list as I did in the original edition of this book but only offer suggestions of things I have found particularly useful.

POTS, PANS, AND BAKEWARE

Someone I know uses two full-size pressure cookers every evening to cook individual portions of two vegetables. She hardly ever uses a double boiler, preferring to stand guard over soup or whatever is heating in a saucepan. Not my style. I have two 3-cup double boilers and one 2-cup size (also a big one for entertaining; see Chapter 17). In these I can heat soup, a main dish such as creamed chicken, and a vegetable. A pressure cooker can handle small amounts successfully and is useful for stews, soups, and long-cooking vegetables such as artichokes. The 4-quart size takes up no more room than the 2½ quart and is more practical, as it can be used for entertaining as well.

Two sizes of skillets—I like the heavy ones made of cast iron and coated with enamel.

A small roasting pan 9 by 9 inches and an even smaller one 7 by 7 have many uses, as does a cookie sheet 12 × 8½ inches.

For baking, a single-serving-size casserole and a two-serving one, with lids. Ovenproof glass or enamel-coated cast iron are equally practical, and perhaps the best are made of pyroceram, which can go from freezer to oven without thawing. A few ovenproof glass custard cups have many uses, as do assorted sizes of mixing bowls.

CUTTING TOOLS

Good cutlery is well worth a little extra money, and an Aladdin sharpener is easiest on the blades. Knives should include a bread knife, vegetable knife, French chopping knife, and grapefruit knife, useful also for oranges, removing seeds from melons, peppers, and acorn squash, and for retrieving can lids that have dropped into the can after opening. Kitchen scissors (get the kind that come apart and can be properly washed, and treat them with respect) should not be used for cutting flowers, opening packages, etc.; keep an old pair of scissors for such chores. A meat grinder has obvious uses, and a Mouli grater will mince vegetables even finer. A chopper that screws into a measuring cup is good for hard-boiled eggs, onions, olives, nuts.

SMALL APPLIANCES

COFFEE MAKER—a matter of individual choice. If you use instant coffee a tea kettle will do for all hot drinks. An electric kettle is useful if you have only a two-burner stove.

TOASTER—probably everyone's first choice. A toaster oven, if space permits, has many uses and saves fuel.

ELECTRIC CAN OPENER—will prevent frequent frustration.

BLENDER—very versatile. It not only mixes drinks from frosted chocolate to frozen daiquiris but chops (nuts, parsley), grates (cheese), pulverizes (bread and cracker crumbs, brown sugar), purées (vegetables, fruits). It does not substitute for a mixer, so you might want a small portable one with several speeds for baking mixtures and some desserts.

JUICER—optional, as is a waffle iron.

BRISKER—great for families in damp climates but too large for most kitchens. If you have a gas oven with a pilot light put a panful of tired crackers or cookies in the oven for a couple of hours without turning on any heat. Likewise warm plates 15 to 20 minutes before a meal.

SKILLET—optional, probably useful only if you have a two-burner stove.

FOOD PROCESSOR—very expensive and takes up a lot of room.

GADGETS

The following are all in constant use in my kitchen:

TIMER—essential even if your stove has one.
EGG SLICER
VEGETABLE SCRAPER
WIRE WHISK
SMALL PANCAKE LIFTER
SLOTTED SPOON
SMALL LADLE
SPATULA—for sandwich spreads

STORAGE

Most staples may be kept on open shelves and will not deteriorate if kept in closed containers.

General Rules for Refrigerator Storage:
Cover everything. Put what is convenient in covered refrigerator dishes, and have a set of waterproof bowl covers for anything put in containers without tops of their own. This is to preserve moisture. Store foods in the following order:

- Milk, cream, and beverages in coldest part, next to freezing unit.
- Fruits, salads, and food cooked with milk in next coldest section.
- Eggs, butter, fresh vegetables next.
- Meat, soup, other leftovers farthest away from cold.

Never put hot food in refrigerator, but store soups, gravies, and vegetables as soon as cooled.

Plastic bags, aluminum foil, plastic wrap, and waxed paper are all useful in preserving food.

Specific rules:

BANANAS—can be refrigerated, but will turn black.

BREAD—keep tightly wrapped in waxed paper or plastic bag, using the crust cut off the end as a cover for the rest of the loaf to keep moisture in. Sliced bread dries out more quickly than unsliced. Keep in refrigerator or freezer to retard staling. English muffins, which mold very quickly, should always be kept in refrigerator.

BREAD CRUMBS—in covered jar; likewise cracker crumbs.

BUTTER OR MARGARINE—tightly wrapped or covered, in refrigerator, away from all foods with odors.

CANNED FOODS—after opening, keep covered, in refrigerator. They taste better if removed from can. Canned soup can be left in the pot, covered, and reheated when wanted.

CAKES—in covered tin box. Applesauce cake and jelly roll will stay fresh longest, angel and sponge next.

CELERY—in refrigerator, wrapped in waxed paper or dipped in ice water and then put in covered refrigerator dish.

CELERY TOPS—can be dried and stored in covered jar, good for soups or fish.

CHEESE—store in covered container in refrigerator. Spreads will keep in their own covered jars. Put packaged varieties in plastic bags. Keep grated cheese refrigerated in a covered jar.

CITRUS FRUIT—lemons, oranges, and grapefruit will keep in a cool dry place; limes should be kept in a closed jar in the refrigerator. Leftover halves can be kept by covering the exposed end with a waterproof bottle cover or waxed paper.

COFFEE—after vacuum tin has been opened, keep it tightly covered with plastic lid.

COOKIES—to keep crisp, put in airtight tin box; to keep soft, in a cookie jar with a piece of bread. Macaroons keep particularly well.

EGGS—will keep better if taken out of their carton and put in a closed container in refrigerator. Leftover whites or yolks should be put in a small container, tightly covered (air causes deterioration). See freezing directions on p. 27.

FATS—will keep indefinitely in tightly covered tin in refrigerator—an old coffee tin is ideal.

FISH—use fresh fish the same day as purchased; rinse in running cold water as soon as it is brought home, wrap in waxed paper, and store in coldest part of refrigerator until time to cook.

FRUIT—if ripe, keep in refrigerator; if not, in cool dry place. Apples will keep longest, and need not be refrigerated. Melons and avocados, if cut in half, can be kept face down on a piece of waxed paper in refrigerator. Berries are very perishable and should always be kept in refrigerator.

JAMS AND JELLIES—store in cool, dry, preferably dark place until opened.

LETTUCE—in refrigerator, either in bag tightly closed, or remove core, dip in ice water, drain, and put in covered dish. It will keep an amazingly long time.

MEAT—keep wrapped in waxed paper in refrigerator. If using up cooked meat, keep it out of the refrigerator only long enough to take what is wanted.

MUSTARD (PREPARED)—will keep better in the refrigerator.

NUTS—keep tightly covered. Use up quickly. Can be frozen.

OLIVE OIL—drain from can and keep in tightly corked bottle in a cool place.

OLIVES—keep enough juice in the bottle to cover what is left and top with a thin film of olive oil.

ONIONS—cool dark place.

PARSLEY—in closed jar in refrigerator.

PICKLES AND RELISHES—cool place.

POTATOES—keep best in cool, ventilated place.

SALAD DRESSING—mayonnaise and French dressing should be kept in refrigerator.

VEGETABLES—raw and uncut, in cool dry place. If cut and partially used, such as cucumber or eggplant, cover exposed end and keep in refrigerator.

WATERCRESS—in closed jar in refrigerator.

WINE—keep red and white wines tightly corked in a cool place; if they go sour, use as vinegar. Sherry will keep indefinitely anywhere.

Cover all dry staples tightly. Never store anything in direct sunlight except unripe fruit.

SOME HELPFUL HINTS

- Cream whips best when very cold and when both the beater and bowl have been chilled.
- Egg whites beat best when at room temperature—take out of the refrigerator half an hour before whipping.
- Egg white will not beat up stiff if the slightest bit of yolk is left in it.
- Less flour is needed to thicken white sauce if homogenized milk is used.
- Cut onions in running cold water to save your fingers from smelling and your eyes from weeping.
- To unmold gelatins, set mold in a pan of hot water for a minute or two, put a plate over the mold, turn plate and mold upside down, and tap gently with a knife.
- If you don't want to fill all the cups in a muffin tin with batter put water in the empty ones.
- If greens are wilted, douse with hot and then cold water, and put in refrigerator until needed.
- Stale bread can be revived by leaving it in a hot oven for a few minutes. This can be repeated several times.
- A wooden spoon can be left in a pan for continuous stirring and will not get hot.
- When melting chocolate, grease the pan lightly and the chocolate will not stick to it.
- When heating milk, first rinse the saucepan in cold water and the milk will not form a film on the pan.
- When measuring molasses or any syrup, first rinse the cup or spoon in cold water to prevent sticking.
- To wash pans used for eggs, dough, sauces, and puddings, let soak in cold water first; pans with syrup or fats, in hot water.
- Use foil to catch drippings under anything broiled.
- Food left in open cans will not spoil, but it will keep its flavor better if transferred to glass jars with screw tops. This is also a good rule for food in cartons which is not used up immediately, such as nuts, shredded coconut, sugar, flour.
- When adding liquid to thin condensed soups or to butter and flour mixture for sauce, add very slowly at first, blending thoroughly with each addition. This will prevent lumps. Using a wire whisk will also help.

- To brown oven-ready rolls, dot lightly with butter before heating.
- Frozen products ready to heat in their own containers will be easier to handle when hot if set in a larger pan or baking dish.
- KP in a small kitchen: put every ingredient away as soon as used; wash up as you go along; have an ample supply of paper towels and soap-impregnated scouring pads; invest in a flexible spray nozzle for the faucet if your sink has no spray attachment.

HERBS

A few notes on herbs: recipes in this book are for *dried* herbs, with the exception of chives, which are always used fresh or frozen. While they add greatly to the flavor of some dishes, they must be used sparingly—better too little than too much. The following are the most commonly used:

BASIL—for all tomato dishes, eggs, cheese, meats, salads, chowder

BAY LEAF—any soup, meat stews

CHIVES—potatoes, fish, eggs, salads, with cream or cottage cheese, vichyssoise

MARJORAM—any soup, eggs, meat (especially lamb)

MINT—lamb, desserts, iced beverages

OREGANO (wild marjoram with a stronger flavor)—meat loaf, roasts, pasta sauces

PARSLEY—practically anything, especially cream soups and sauces

ROSEMARY—pork and veal, stuffed peppers, eggplant

SAGE—pork, veal, poultry, sausage, fish, stuffed baked potatoes

TARRAGON—eggs, fish, mayonnaise, meat, green salad

THYME—meat, poultry, fish, chowders, stews, bean soup, codfish cakes, meat loaf, curried lamb, eggs

USES FOR LEFTOVER
INGREDIENTS

ANCHOVIES—salads, sandwiches, eggs

BREAD—crumbs, melba or French toast, scalloped dishes, croutons (see p. 147)

COCONUT (shredded or flaked)—curries, frosting, pudding mixes, fruit cup

COFFEE—jelly, puddings

CRACKER CRUMBS—topping for scalloped dishes

CREAM—many desserts, with fruit, cream mayonnaise

EGG WHITES—dessert whips, meringues, frostings, soufflés, sherbets

EGG YOLKS—custard, hollandaise, scrambled eggs

LEMON—sauce, pudding, apple desserts, garnish on fish or soup, iced beverages

OLIVES—sandwiches, potato salad, Spanish omelet, tossed salads, with cottage cheese for dips

NUTS—almonds on fish or green beans; salads, sandwiches, desserts; use promptly, as the natural oils soon produce a stale flavor; can be frozen

PIMIENTO—salad, sandwiches, chicken, tuna or eggs à la king

SOUR CREAM—borscht, on fruit, on gingerbread, madrilène

For other leftovers, see individual foods.

SOME RECOMMENDED
PREPARED PRODUCTS

SEASONED BREAD CRUMBS—use not only for poultry stuffing but also for meat loaf, casserole topping, and on broiled tomatoes.

FRIED ONION RINGS—add to canned hash when heating; makes a nice crunchy topping for creamed baked dishes.

INSTANT ONION AND GARLIC.

INSTANT MASHED POTATOES.

INSTANT ICED TEA—add some lemon juice if too sweet.

INSTANT COFFEE—good for flavoring as well as for hot or iced.

CHEESE (Cheddar type)—available both grated and diced, in pliofilm bags; the processed soft spread in jars is too bland for sandwiches or crackers but is useful when melted cheese is wanted for sauce or topping.

CHEESE SLICES—useful for sandwiches or for making julienne slivers for salads.

LEMON OR LIME JUICE—concentrated in plastic squeeze containers shaped and colored like the fruit; use one-half the amount of fresh juice specified in recipe.

PUDDING AND GELATIN MIXES—instant and low-calorie varieties are available as well as the regular ones.

SAUCES—meat and clam sauces for spaghetti; regular tomato sauce has more flavor than condensed tomato soup for meat loaf, stuffed peppers, etc., but try condensed cream of celery, cream of chicken, cream of mushroom, and Cheddar cheese soups for other shortcuts.

3

———— ✿ ————

THE FREEZER

WHEN I FIRST WROTE this book, and for many years thereafter, I lived in a small rent-controlled apartment where the landlord was not providing any luxuries. My poorly insulated refrigerator held only two small ice trays—if you took one out, you could store one package of frozen vegetables and no more. Keeping even a small amount of ice cream took some ingenuity, and even then it was apt to be mushy. Moving to a larger apartment with a fully equipped kitchen was a revelation after years of makeshifts. Most welcome was a small freezer above the refrigerator with a separate door, not big enough to hold a turkey but more than adequate for my needs. With this storage space I now market once a week, not on the dead run to the nearest store after a day's work, but on the weekend, with enough time—and a handy pushcart—to try more distant markets and do some comparative shopping.

One of the best uses to which a live-aloner can put the freezer is to store leftover stew, casseroles, and meat loaf. It can be convenient and often economical to cook larger quantities and after using two or three servings to store the rest. In this way something tasty and filling will be on hand for emergencies or times when you don't feel like cooking. I always seem to have potatoes and gravy left over from stews which I purée in the blender and mix with a can of diluted onion soup. This makes a hearty potage which can be frozen and used as wanted.

A freezing compartment in the refrigerator, without a separate door, will not keep foods as long as a separate freezer, but this is much better than nothing. To keep frozen foods fresh for the longest period of time, the temperature must be 0° F. or below. A small refrigerator thermometer will be an inexpensive asset, or two if your freezer and refrigerator are separate.

GENERAL RULES

- Chill well before freezing, either before or after packaging. Discard the market wrappings and use pliofilm, plastic, heavy-duty foil or sturdy containers. Containers of dairy food —cottage cheese, yogurt, etc.—are not heavy enough.
- Don't overcook main dishes, and remove from heat immediately to prevent further cooking.
- Pasta and vegetables should be cooked *al dente* so that they won't get mushy when frozen.

UNCOOKED FOOD

- Meat, poultry, or seafood should be wrapped in heavy-duty foil. Discard the thin plastic and cardboard in which they are sold. Label and date each package.
- Chops or small steaks: wrap separately in waxed paper, then overwrap with foil. Will last 3 to 4 months.
- Ground meat: wrap patties separately, then overwrap. Will last 2 to 3 months.
- Poultry: wrap pieces separately. Will last up to 12 months.
- Bacon, sausage, frankfurters: use within 1 month.
- Chicken livers: package in single servings. Will last up to 6 months.
- Variety meats can be frozen but not as successfully as the above.
- Shrimp, in the shell or peeled, will last up to 6 months.
- Scallops: freeze raw; defrost in refrigerator until they can be separated. Will last up to 4 months.
- Clams and oysters: remove from shells; drain well. Will last up to 6 months.

COOKED FOOD

- Use plastic, tin, or aluminum containers with tightly fitting tops.
- Some heatproof dishes can go directly from the freezer to the oven, but not to stove-top or broiler, while those of pyroceram can be used with any heat. Check manufacturers' directions.
- Label and date on a piece of adhesive tape.
- Stews will last 2 to 3 months.
- Meat loaf will last up to 3 months.
- Lobster meat will last up to 2 months.
- Crab meat will last up to 3 months.

MISCELLANEOUS

- Form cookie dough into rolls for easy slicing when only partially defrosted. Will keep up to 6 months.
- Sandwiches should be kept no longer than 1 month. Do not freeze lettuce or tomatoes. Mayonnaise is apt to separate, so use butter. See p. 155 for flavored butters.
- Nuts will keep fresh much longer in the freezer. Store in plastic bags or containers. Unopened vacuum-packed nuts need not be frozen.
- Cheese packed in freezer wrap will keep for several months, but use promptly when removing from freezer. If someone gives you a box of assorted cheeses or a large single cheese, freeze some portions.
- Parsley; when perfectly dry, snip the leaves from the stems, chop in the blender, and store in a wide-mouth screw-top jar.
- Herbs and celery leaves can be left whole, stored in plastic bags, and cut as needed.
- Orange and lemon rind, with no pulp attached, can be wrapped in heavy foil and frozen. Grate while still frozen.
- It is possible, although not particularly recommended, to freeze a partly used container of milk (liquids expand on freezing). If using up milk is a problem, consider dry milk,

which can be mixed in small quantities—an opened package should not be kept beyond 6 months.

- Egg whites can be frozen and if you put each one in a separate ice-cube container you will know exactly how many you have. (See p. 22 for uses.)
- Leftover cooked rice can be frozen. Thaw in boiling water and drain before reheating over steam or in a double boiler. Will keep approximately 1 month.
- If you cannot spare a casserole dish, line it with foil, fill with food, and freeze. Lift out the foil package and keep frozen until wanted. Then put it back in the dish, defrost, and heat.
- Date all packages and label those in opaque wrapping or containers. Post a list on the freezer door.

Keep on hand extra concentrated fruit juice, 2 or 3 packages of frozen vegetables, some commercially prepared main dishes such as chicken pie or lasagna, 2 or 3 pints of ice cream. Then if an unexpected guest turns up or you are housed with a cold or because of bad weather, you will be prepared. You might make some of your favorite dishes to have on hand in the event of a busy week with little time for cooking.

If you have a garden or are near a farmers' market or a good roadside stand, take advantage of fresh produce at its best—and cheapest—and freeze some of it. However, if you have the space and the time to go in for freezing in a big way, invest in a specialized book on the subject.

4

❧

MENUS

ONE-COURSE MEALS may consist of two dishes which can be eaten together and which will give a good balance of proteins and carbohydrates, such as a cheese or egg dish with a salad; a soup and a sandwich; or a salad and a sandwich. For instance:

Cheese Soufflé · Green Bean Salad

Baked Gnocchi · Asparagus Salad

Creamed Eggs and Ham or Anchovy on Toast
Mixed Vegetable Salad

Poached Eggs Plus · Tossed Green Salad

Black Bean Soup · Chopped Tuna and Celery Sandwich

Cream of Spinach Soup · Liverwurst and Lettuce Sandwich

Tomato Soup · Chopped Chicken Livers and Bacon
Sandwich

Corn Chowder · Tomato and Cucumber Sandwich

Ham or Bologna on Corn-Molasses Bread ·
Cole Slaw with Grated Carrots and Green Pepper

Tongue and Rye Bread Sandwich ·
Vegetable Salad with Russian Dressing

Cream Cheese Sandwich on Brown Bread ·
Grapefruit Salad with French Dressing

Chopped Egg Sandwich on Whole Wheat Bread ·
Potato Salad with Chives

Toasted Cheese Sandwich · Chicory and Endive Salad

Two-course meals may consist of a filling soup with a light salad or fruit; a casserole combination with a salad or dessert; or a light soup and a substantial salad. Here are some suggestions:

New England Clam Chowder · Banana and Orange Slices

Cream of Chicken Soup · Celery and Apple Salad

Oyster Stew with Paprika ·
Pineapple and Cream Cheese Salad with Tart French Dressing

Vegetable-Beef Soup · French Toast with Ginger Marmalade

Scrambled Eggs with Chipped Beef · Peach and Cottage
Cheese Salad

Cream of Shrimp Soup · Avocado and Grapefruit Salad ·
Toasted Cheese Crackers

Asparagus Soufflé · Peaches Baked with Orange Marmalade

Tuna à la King · Fresh Fruit and Cookies

Double Decker Sandwich · Tapioca with Raspberry-Applesauce

Three-course meals generally consist of a soup or appetizer, a main course with vegetables, and a dessert. With more dishes, it is easier to arrange a good nutritional balance. The twelve menu suggestions that follow give ideas in the second column for using up some leftovers next day, adding a new dish for variety.

MENU SUGGESTIONS

FIRST DAY	SECOND DAY

Tomato Juice
Curried Shrimp and Rice
  with Chutney
Green Beans
Berries and Cream
	Shrimp and Cauliflower
	  Casserole au Gratin
	Green Bean Salad
	Cupcake with Hot Berry
	  Sauce

Hot or Jellied Bouillon
Boiled Lobster with Melted
  Butter
Carrot and Celery Sticks,
  Potato Chips
Blueberries and Cream
	Cream of Carrot Soup
	Lobster Salad
	Blueberry Tart

Borscht, Hot or Cold Lamb Chop, Mint Jelly Creamed Spinach Shoestring Potatoes Prune Whip	Eggs Florentine Buttered Beets Lemon Pudding

Chicken Gumbo
Eggs Benedict
Artichoke with Hollandaise
Gingerbread and Chocolate
    Sauce

Ham with Currant Jelly
Cold Artichoke and
    Mayonnaise
Fruit Cup and Gingerbread

Turkey Noodle Soup
Kedgeree
Peas Bonne Femme
Pears with Jam and
    Custard

Cream of Pea Soup
Cold Salmon Mayonnaise
Shortbread Custard

Apple Juice
Rice Supreme
Asparagus Tips
Coffee Jelly

Sautéed Kidneys with Rice
Asparagus Salad
Coffee Whip

Tomato and Clam Juice
    Cocktail
Scrambled Eggs on
    Anchovy Toast
Creamed Cucumbers
Apricot Whip

Tomato Bouillon
Baked Fillet of Flounder
Sliced Cucumbers with
    French Dressing
Fruit Compote with Sherry

Mushroom Soup
New England Fish Cakes
Cole Slaw
Baked Apple with Nuts
    and Raisins

Corned Beef Hash
Cabbage au Gratin
Apple Betty

Clam Juice
Ham Steak
Stuffed Baked Potato
Broccoli
Fruit Shortcake

Ham Omelet
Broccoli Baked in Cheese
    Sauce
Trifle

Vegetable Soup
Fried Sausage and Apple
    Rings
Boiled Hominy and Butter
Chocolate Icebox Cake

Veal Chop with Brown
    Gravy
Baked Grits
Lime Fruit Jelly

———

Bouillon on the Rocks
Broiled Cheeseburgers with
    Broiled Tomato
Tossed Green Salad
Spiced Baked Pears

Meat Loaf with Mushroom
    Sauce
Lima Beans
Pear and Cream Cheese
    Salad

———

Cranberry Juice
Risotto with Mushrooms
Buttered Zucchini
Broiled Grapefruit

Omelet with Chopped
    Mushroom Stems
Green Peas
Half Grapefruit with
    Sherry

SOME COLD-WEATHER MENUS

Cream of Spinach Soup · Sausage and Mushroom Casserole ·
Baked Bananas

———

Vegetable-Juice Cocktail · Baked Ham ·
Baked Sweet Potato ·
Corn Pudding · Grapefruit

———

Cream of Tomato Soup · Scalloped Fish ·
Green Beans au Gratin · Prune Whip

———

Onion Soup · Cheese Soufflé · Tossed Green Salad ·
Gingerbread with Chocolate Sauce

———

Cream of Celery Soup ·
Baked Beans with Bacon and Brown Bread ·
Sliced Tomatoes with French Dressing · Baked Custard

Oyster Stew · Vegetable Salad · Toasted Cheese Crackers ·
Coffee Éclair

Clam-Juice Cocktail · Stuffed Peppers · Glazed Carrots ·
Cupcake with Lemon Sauce

Minestrone with Grated Parmesan . · Green Salad ·
Bel Paese Cheese and Crusty French Bread · Fruit ·
Espresso Coffee

Hot Vegetable Juice · Chicken Baked in White Wine ·
Brown Rice ·
Romaine Lettuce with Blue Cheese Dressing ·
Lemon Meringue Tart

SOME HOT-WEATHER MENUS

Jellied Bouillon · Broiled Liver and Creamed Potatoes ·
Grapes with Mint

Hot Purée Mongole · Jellied Pâté Salad · Cake with Hot
Fruit Sauce

Cold Purée Mongole · Soft-Shell Crabs ·
Sliced Cucumbers with French Dressing · Berries and Cream

Vichyssoise · Ham with Currant Jelly · Zucchini ·
Peaches and Cream

*Jellied Bouillon · Seafood Newburg · Endive Salad ·
Cantaloupe with Sherry*

Vegetable Juice · Poached Eggs Plus · Coffee Ice Cream

Madrilène · Curried Shrimp and Rice · Fruit Compote

---

*Egg in Aspic · Fresh Asparagus with Hollandaise Sauce ·
Banana Custard*

---

*Chicken Bouillon with Rice · Summer Salad ·
Pineapple Sherbet*

A nice variation for hot weather is a simple version of smorgasbord—stuffed eggs, potato salad, sliced tomatoes, sardines, olives, liver pâté—any or all of these—and pumpernickel. Follow with a hot dessert such as apple betty or cake with a hot, sweet sauce.

Breads, beverages, and salad (if not specified) are of course optional with all these meals.

SOME TRAY SUPPERS

Clam Stew with Toasted Crackers · Fruit Salad

Welsh Rabbit on Toasted English Muffin · Fruit Cup

Black Bean Soup with Hard-Boiled Egg · Half Grapefruit

---

*Vegetable Soup · Buttered Toast · Rice Pudding with
Quinces*

---

*Chicken and Noodle Soup · Applesauce with Cinnamon
Graham Crackers*

Scalloped Cheese · Green Salad

Chicken Broth · Avocado and Grapefruit Salad · Date-Nut Bread with Cream Cheese

---

Cheese Omelet · Fresh Fruit

For one-dish soup meals, see p. 46. Occasionally there comes a day when one has no appetite but must eat something—try a bowl of onion soup combined with slices of toast and grated Parmesan cheese. It is wonderfully reviving.

MINUTE MEALS IN THE BLENDER

- 1 egg, ½ cup orange juice, ½ cup cold milk, 1 jar baby-food bananas or 1 ripe banana, sliced
- 1 egg, ½ can tomato soup, 1 cup cold milk, dash of nutmeg
- 1 egg, 1 cup cold milk, 1 teaspoon instant coffee, sugar to taste
- 1 egg, 1 cup cold milk, ½ cup sliced fruit or berries, sugar to taste
- 1 egg yolk, ¾ cup orange juice, 1 tablespoon wheat germ

LUNCH TO GO

The obvious choices are sandwiches, a container of yogurt or cottage cheese, fresh fruit in season, and some cookies. Don't forget hard-boiled eggs, which are more interesting if deviled. Invest in a small wide-mouth thermos jar and use it for hearty soups and even stews; also for salad combinations, but omit lettuce—it will get limp if packed with dressing. Try cottage cheese topped with sliced fruit—canned is juicier—and a sprinkle of sesame seeds. If your office water cooler has a hot water tap use it for an envelope of dehydrated soup as well as for coffee or tea.

LUNCH AT HOME

Soup, sandwiches, and salads are standbys but can become monotonous. If eggs were not served for breakfast try some of the egg and cheese dishes in Chapter 6. Or if dry cereal was not a breakfast choice combine your favorite with a sliced banana, fresh peach, or berries. Some form of pasta is good for lunch, but be sure to include a green vegetable or a glass of mixed vegetable juice. Other suggestions are sautéed mushrooms and bacon on toast, an artichoke with hollandaise sauce, creamed chicken, chipped beef or fish on toast.

5

─────────── ❧ ───────────

SOUPS

Soup is an excellent way to begin any meal, as a light first course to a dinner, hot or cold according to season; as the hot dish to accompany a sandwich or salad in a lighter meal; or as a one-dish meal in itself. Contrary to the general impression, many kinds of soup can be made quite easily, starting from the soup kettle. For a minimum of effort use the canned variety. Either kind can be dressed up in a number of ways:

- With a pinch of dried herbs—rosemary to pea, celery, and asparagus soups; tarragon to all chicken soups; basil to all tomato soups; thyme to bean soups; dill to clam chowders and potato soups.
- With a sprinkling of chopped fresh parsley or paprika when ready to serve—especially good on pale cream soups.
- By adding sherry to a clear meat stock such as consommé or turtle soup (do not add until ready to serve).
- By adding cooked leftover rice or spaghetti to clear soups.
- With a spoonful of whipped cream on tomato soup or clam broth, or sour cream on borscht.
- With grated cheese on vegetable or onion soup.
- With croutons—particularly good on cream of tomato or pea soup (see p. 147).

Soup made from meat is likely to be too much trouble for one person, involving a number of ingredients and longer time than cream soups; also, it should be made in fairly large proportions which are difficult to reduce, but a tasty cup of broth can easily be made from the bones of a broiler or a Rock Cornish hen. Cream soups are easy, quick, and practicable, and can be made one cup at a time if desired, although it is more sensible to make two servings and have enough for the following day.

Cream Soup

1 tablespoon butter
1 small onion, minced
1 teaspoon chopped fresh celery leaves
1 tablespoon flour
1 cup milk, or ½ cup milk and ½ cup vegetable cooking
    water
1 cup cooked vegetable, mashed or strained,
    salt and pepper

Melt butter, add onion and celery, and cook slowly for 10 minutes. Blend in flour and when well mixed add liquid slowly, stirring constantly. Add the cooked vegetable and season with salt and pepper. Mix well and heat thoroughly, stirring frequently unless double boiler is used.

Vegetables suitable for cream soup are carrots, cauliflower, asparagus, peas, mushrooms, celery, potatoes, onions, tomatoes, lima beans, corn, spinach. They are generally chopped fine, mashed, or strained before adding.

Bisque can be made following this recipe, substituting seafood for the vegetables and using more seasoning. This makes 2 servings. An electric blender will make wonderful cream soups from leftovers and will combine canned condensed soups better than hand mixing.

CANNED SOUPS

The usual can size makes two servings. Leftover soup can be kept in the saucepan, covered, and put in the refrigerator when cool. Half a can of condensed cream soup, especially tomato, mushroom, or cream of chicken, can be saved and used as the basis for a sauce. To condensed soups add an equal amount of water if it is a meat stock, or cream or milk if purée (pea or tomato). Save the water used in cooking vegetables and use it with either kind. Many varieties of canned soup are on the market, all excellent on the whole, and most of them are even better when flavored a bit according to taste. For instance:

BLACK BEAN—add 1 tablespoon sherry or a slice of lemon.
CHICKEN OR TURKEY NOODLE—add a dash of curry powder.
CONSOMMÉ—add 1 tablespoon sherry or a slice of lemon.
MUSHROOM—add 1 teaspoon Worcestershire sauce or 1 teaspoon sherry.
PEA—add a bouillon cube while cooking; dissolve thoroughly.
TOMATO—add a pinch of dried basil or curry powder.

Other varieties easily found are asparagus, beef, bean and bacon, clam chowder, cream of chicken, chicken gumbo, cream of vegetable, turkey, Scotch broth, turtle, vegetable, minestrone. Many cookbooks list combinations of two or more canned soups, which add variety to the menu but double the quantity. If you don't mind the same soup for more than two servings you might experiment. Or you can freeze leftovers.

A quick cup of broth can be made by adding a bouillon cube to tomato or mixed vegetable juice. Clam juice from cans or bottles can be heated to make broth, either alone or in equal parts with tomato juice. Canned baby foods can be mixed with milk and used as soup, but they need considerable seasoning if none is used in their production.

Real New England fish and clam chowders are available in cans, as well as cream of lobster, cream of shrimp, and oyster stew. These soups average two portions per can and in most cases must be diluted with milk, not water.

Dehydrated soups come in aluminum foil envelopes which are ideal for storing, as they take up much less room than cans. Each envelope yields three generous portions, and at least 15 minutes is necessary for simmering these soups so that all the ingredients become thoroughly softened. Instant dehydrated soups in individual envelopes (one serving) are available in many varieties. Just add boiling water, stir, and serve.

Good as canned soups are, they can become monotonous. Watch for new varieties, not only in the familiar brands but for new brands as well.

Borscht

Dilute one can of consommé as directed and add one jar of baby-food strained beets, ½ teaspoon instant onion, and salt to taste. Serve with a spoonful of sour cream as topping, sprinkled with a little chopped parsley.

Lima Bean Soup

Mash thoroughly 1 cup cooked lima beans. Add 1½ cups milk, a pinch of onion flakes, a pinch of dried sage, and a chicken bouillon cube. Heat over a low flame until cube is dissolved and mixture is simmering. Stir frequently; do not boil. Add salt and pepper if necessary.

Corn Chowder

Dilute a can of condensed cream of chicken soup according to directions and combine with a small can of niblet corn, drained. Season with Worcestershire sauce and a dash of chili powder. Purée in blender if desired. Leftover succotash can be used the same way. If serving chilled, add a dash of curry powder.

Cream of Spinach Soup

Make a thin white sauce with 1 tablespoon butter, 1 tablespoon flour, and 1 cup milk. Dissolve a chicken bouillon cube in this, and season with salt, pepper, and a dash each of onion salt, celery salt, and nutmeg or mace. Blend in one jar of baby-food strained spinach.

Cream of Carrot Soup

Make in the same way as Cream of Spinach, but use a beef bouillon cube and for seasoning a pinch each of thyme and savory as well as salt and pepper. Blend in one jar of baby-food strained carrots.

Oyster Stew

    1½ tablespoons butter
     1 teaspoon Worcestershire sauce
    ½ teaspoon paprika
    ¼ teaspoon salt
      pinch of black pepper
    ½ cup milk
    ½ cup cream
6 or 8 oysters

Melt 1 tablespoon butter and stir in seasonings. Add the liquor from the oysters, milk, and cream; and, when this begins to bubble, add the oysters, stirring slowly. When the oysters are plump and the edges begin to curl, pour into a bowl and add the rest of the butter.

Clam Stew

Drain the liquid from a small can of minced clams and bring this to a boil with 1 tablespoon butter. Season with celery salt and paprika. Add ½ cup light cream and bring to a boil. Add the clams and heat for a very few seconds—overcooking makes the clams tough.

Clam Soup

Combine 1 cup clam juice with ¼ cup heavy cream. Heat, but *do not boil.* Season with celery salt and white pepper. Sprinkle minced parsley on top.

Mushroom Broth

Take the caps from an 8-ounce box of small button mushrooms and slice very thin. Sauté in 3 tablespoons butter with 1 teaspoon instant onion until the mushrooms are juicy. Add 1 can chicken broth and bring just to the boil. Test for seasoning. Add 1 table-spoon sherry before serving. Makes 2 generous, 3 medium serv-ings.

Escarole Soup

Cook the outside leaves of a head of escarole in boiling salted water until tender. Drain, and chop very fine in the blender to measure about 1½ tablespoons. In a bowl, beat 1 egg. Add the escarole and 1 tablespoon grated Parmesan cheese. Heat 3 cups beef broth to boiling and gradually add the escarole and cheese mixture. Serve at once. Makes 3–4 servings.

Zucchini Soup

1 small onion, chopped
1 tablespoon butter
2 cups chicken broth
2 small zucchini, diced
1 tablespoon chopped parsley
  thyme
  celery salt
  pepper
  plain yogurt

Sauté the onion in butter until soft. Add broth, zucchini, parsley, and a dash of thyme. Simmer until the zucchini is soft, then add celery salt and pepper and purée in the blender. Serve hot or cold, with a spoonful of plain yogurt. Makes 2-3 servings.

Blender Salad Soup

Mix 1 cup chicken broth or beef consommé with 1½ teaspoons flour. Put in the blender. Add 2 cups leftover mixed green salad, dressing and all. Purée until smooth. Cook very slowly until it thickens, stirring constantly. Serve with garlic-flavored croutons or grated cheese or both. Makes 1–2 servings.

Chicken Broth

Put the bones from a broiled chicken or a Rock Cornish hen in a saucepan with enough water to cover, about 1½ cups. Add 1 teaspoon each of onion and celery flakes. Season with salt and pepper. Simmer, covered, over low heat for 45 minutes. Allow to cool and skim off fat. Remove bones and reheat, or refrigerate and use as jellied consommé.

COLD SOUPS

Excellent varieties are available in cans, the most usual being beef consommé, chicken consommé, and tomato consommé (madrilène). These must be left in the refrigerator, either in the can or a bowl, for 4 or 5 hours to jell, and so require a little forethought. Serve with a wedge of lemon and chopped fresh parsley. Madrilène is delicious broken up with a fork and a dab of sour cream put on top. In general jellied soups need more flavoring than hot soups. Chilled creamed soups are equally good in hot weather but must be served very cold and highly seasoned. **Purée Mongole** (1 can condensed tomato soup, 1 can condensed pea soup, and 1 can milk—also good hot) needs Worcestershire sauce and cayenne pepper. Canned gazpacho is available in some markets.

Cold Tomato Soup I

Add 1 cup light cream and 1 teaspoon curry powder to 1 can of uncondensed tomato soup. Chill in refrigerator.

Cold Tomato Soup II

Peel one very ripe large tomato (or two small ones) and put through the meat grinder directly into a serving bowl. Add a little minced onion, salt, and pepper; chill. To serve, top with a generous spoonful of mayonnaise strongly flavored with curry powder.

Vichyssoise

Dilute condensed cream of potato soup as directed and mix in the blender. Serve well chilled and top with chopped chives. After trying many kinds of canned vichyssoise, I have found this comes nearest to the real thing.

Jellied Herb Consommé

Soften 1 tablespoon gelatin in 1 tablespoon water. Add 2 cups consommé, 1 tablespoon sherry, and ½ teaspoon each of parsley, chives, and chervil. Allow to jell and serve with slightly salted whipped cream. Makes 2-3 servings.

Or use chicken broth, madeira, rosemary, chives, and parsley. Add a touch of curry powder to the cream.

Senegalese Soup

Combine 1 can condensed cream of chicken soup with 1 container (10¾ oz., or about 1⅓ cups) of half-and-half. Simmer. Just before it boils stir in ½ teaspoon curry powder and the juice of 1 lemon. Bring just to the boil, remove from heat, and chill. Serve very cold with very thin slices of cucumber or chopped chives. Makes 2-3 servings.

Quick Gazpacho

Mix ½ cup white bread crumbs, not too fine, with 4 cups tomato juice. Grate 1 medium-size or 2 small white onions. Add to the juice and heat to boiling. Chill, then season well with Tabasco, salt, and pepper. Add 5 or 6 thin slices of cucumber to each serving. Makes 3-4 servings.

Green Gazpacho

Put in the blender 2 small peeled tomatoes, 3 stalks celery, chopped, 1 small cucumber, peeled and diced, 3 or 4 leaves romaine or other lettuce, ¼ cup orange juice, 2 or 3 scallions, and some parsley. Blend until well mixed; serve very cold. Serves 2.

Avocado Soup

Peel 1 ripe avocado and dice into small pieces. Blend with 1 cup heavy cream until smooth. Season with salt and pepper and chill. Serves 2.

Cold Cucumber Soup

1 can (10½ oz.) clear chicken broth
1 small cucumber, peeled, seeded, and diced
½ cup yogurt
¼ teaspoon dried dill
½ teaspoon grated lemon rind
salt and pepper

Bring soup to a boil. Add cucumber and simmer 10 minutes. Cool. Mix in the blender, add yogurt, and blend. Stir in seasonings. Chill thoroughly. Makes 2 generous servings.

ONE-DISH MEALS

Filling soups such as Scotch broth, pepperpot, bean and bacon, and chowders are suitable; probably you will want to eat the whole can in a big bowl with crackers or toast. Black bean soup can be augmented with a chopped hard-boiled egg; pea soup with two or three cut-up frankfurters; spinach soup with crab meat; mushroom soup with tuna fish; meat soup with rice and vegetables. A can of minestrone is a meal in itself, but you may add any cooked leftovers—vegetables, meat, spaghetti; serve with plenty of grated Parmesan or Romano cheese and Italian bread sticks.

6

---⟡---

EGGS AND CHEESE

EGG DISHES

EGGS are one of the most satisfactory sources of protein for single meals and an excellent alternative to meat or fish for the main course. They will keep a long time if stored in a cool place and present no leftover problems. *Strictly* fresh eggs are best for boiling or poaching. If you have any doubts about freshness put the egg in a bowl of water; if it sinks it is still fresh. Unless you wear out your taste for eggs by using them as breakfast food, you will find that they can be served in a large number of ways, either alone or combined with other foods. Bacon, ham, and chicken livers are very good with poached, shirred, fried, or scrambled eggs; also little sausages or broiled tomato halves.

Hard-Boiled Eggs

Place in cold water, bring to a boil, reduce heat, and simmer for 12 to 15 minutes. Hold under cold water a few minutes before removing the shell. For salads or deviled eggs, chill for at least an hour before shelling, as the eggs will then peel much more easily. Use hard-boiled eggs in the following ways:

- Sliced, in white sauce, on toast, either plain or spread with deviled ham.
- Sliced or whole, in curry sauce with rice.
- À la king, in cream sauce with mushrooms and pimientos.
- Chopped with mayonnaise in sandwiches.
- In salad, either plain or deviled.

Hard-Boiled Egg Casserole

Dice 1 large or 2 small cold cooked potatoes and combine with two hard-boiled eggs, diced. Put in a greased baking dish with 1 cup of medium white sauce (p. 141), season with salt and pepper, and bake in a 350° F. oven for 15 minutes. For the last 5 minutes put on top of the dish 2 slices of bacon which have been lightly fried and drained of fat.

Deviled Eggs

Cut a hard-boiled egg in half lengthwise and remove the yolk, being careful not to break the white. Put the yolk in a bowl, mash with a fork, and add 2 or 3 tablespoons cream, enough to make a soft paste. Season with salt, cayenne pepper, a dash of dry mustard, and freshly chopped chives or a pinch of dried herbs. Or you can soften the yolk with mayonnaise and add ⅛ teaspoon curry powder. When mixed put back in the whites. Use cold as an appetizer or with salad. Or put in a baking dish, cover with white sauce, top with bread crumbs dotted with butter or with grated cheese, and bake until lightly browned in a 350° F. oven for about 15 minutes. Use at least 2 eggs, even for one serving.

Coddled Eggs

These require a special little china pot with a screw-on metal top. Grease the inside with butter or margarine, slide in the raw egg, add salt and pepper, and screw the top on firmly. Submerge in boiling water and cook for 6 minutes.

Eggs Florentine

Put ½ cup cooked, finely chopped spinach in a shallow greased baking dish, break an egg on top of the spinach, and sprinkle with salt and pepper and grated cheese. Bake in a 350° F. oven for 15 minutes.

Baked Egg and Tomato

Scald a tomato in boiling water, plunge into cold water, and remove the skin. Cut a hollow center in it, removing the seeds and pulp. Drop in a raw egg and season with salt, pepper, thyme, basil, and grated cheese. Put in a shallow greased baking dish and bake in a 350° F. oven 20 minutes.

Baked Eggs with Cheese and Yogurt

Butter a shallow individual baking dish and cover the bottom with grated Parmesan cheese. Break 1 or 2 eggs over the cheese and cover them with plain yogurt. Season with salt and pepper. Sprinkle with more cheese and dot with butter. Bake 15 minutes at 350° F. Eat from the dish or on toast.

Eggs in Nests

Carefully separate 2 eggs. Beat the whites until stiff and put in a greased individual baking dish. Make two depressions in the egg white and slide one yolk into each one. Season with salt, pepper, and paprika. Bake 10 minutes at 350° F., until the yolks are set and the white delicately brown. Sprinkle with parsley if desired.

Cheese Eggs

Melt 1 tablespoon butter in an individual baking dish. Put in 2 slices Gruyère cheese cut to fit the dish. Cook in a slow to moderate oven until the cheese begins to bubble. Carefully break 2 eggs over the cheese, season with salt and pepper, and cook until set.

Poached Eggs

Fill a frying pan three-quarters full of water. Bring to a boil, reduce heat, and let the water simmer. Add 1 tablespoon vinegar or ¼ teaspoon salt to keep the white from spreading or use a muffin ring in which to drop the egg. Slide the egg in gently, cover, and cook until the white is almost firm. Take out carefully with a pancake lifter. An individual poacher is even easier to use.

Serve on toast with cream, tomato, or cheese sauce. Or serve on corned beef hash, scrapple, or cooked ham.

Eggs Benedict

Split and toast an English muffin, put a thin slice of cooked ham (heated) on each half, then add the poached eggs and cover with hollandaise sauce which has been warmed in a small double boiler.

Poached Eggs Plus

Split an English muffin and toast both halves lightly. Put on each half a slice of American cheese, a slice of tomato, and a strip of bacon, cut in half. Place under the broiler and cook until the bacon is browned. While this is cooking, poach 2 eggs and when done put them on top of the bacon. This is so good that you will have no trouble eating both halves.

Shirred Eggs

Butter a small individual baking dish. Break into it 1 or 2 eggs, and add 1 tablespoon cream, salt, and pepper. Bake in 350° F. oven 15 minutes until white is set and yolk is still soft. Sautéed chicken livers or tiny sausages can be added when serving.

Scrambled Eggs

Melt 1 teaspoon butter in a small frying pan over very low heat; do not let the pan get hot. Mix in a bowl 2 eggs with salt, white pepper, and two drops of Tabasco, and if you like your eggs creamy 2 tablespoons milk or cream. Pour into the buttered pan and cook over low heat, stirring gently and continuously with a fork until almost cooked. Remove from the heat and stir a few more minutes—the heat in the pan will finish the cooking. Best results are obtained by using low heat and giving the eggs your undivided attention.

Serve plain or on toast, or on toast spread with anchovy paste or deviled ham; or serve in a ring of spinach mixed with thin white sauce.

Add the chopped stems from ½ pound mushrooms—they will cook in the eggs.

Add ¼ cup chipped beef, finely shredded, to the mixture before scrambling. Use less salt, however, as the beef is already salty.

For lunch or supper, try scrambling the eggs with 2 heaping tablespoons cottage cheese, either plain or with chives. (Omit milk or cream.)

French Omelet

Heat a small frying pan and when hot rub some salt over it with a paper towel before starting to cook the eggs. Remove the salt. Mix in a bowl 2 eggs, 2 tablespoons milk, salt, and pepper. Melt a teaspoon of butter in the hot pan and pour in the eggs. With a spatula keep loosening the mixture from the edge as it cooks and tilt the pan slightly so that the uncooked part runs along the edge. When still a little soft in the middle, fold over with a pancake lifter and take out carefully.

OMELET AUX FINES HERBES

Add 1 teaspoon mixed herbs to eggs.

CHEESE OMELET

Add 2 tablespoons grated cheese to eggs.

HAM OMELET

Add 2 tablespoons minced ham to eggs.

SPANISH OMELET

Serve the omelet with a sauce made by stewing together for 10 minutes 2 slices of skinned tomato, 4 or 5 stuffed olives, sliced, 1 or 2 mushrooms, sliced, and 1 tablespoon each of minced green pepper and minced onion. Cook in enough water to keep ingredients from sticking. Season and serve over the omelet.

SWEET OMELET

When egg mixture is ready to fold, put 2 tablespoons of hot jam in the middle. Fold and dust lightly with powdered sugar.

Fried Eggs

Melt 2 tablespoons butter or bacon fat in a very small pan. When hot, slide in 1 or 2 eggs, broken into a saucer. Flick in a few drops of water. Cover, reduce heat, and cook gently until just firm on top. Serve with slices of fried scrapple, ham, or Canadian bacon.

Eggs Beurre Noire

In a small saucepan melt 1 tablespoon butter; add 1½ teaspoons vinegar, ½ teaspoon salt, a dash of pepper, and 2 teaspoons chopped parsley. Melt a second tablespoon butter in a ramekin and fry 1 or 2 eggs to your taste. Pour the browned butter mixture over the eggs and serve.

French Toast

Trim the crusts from 3 slices of white bread. Beat 1 egg in ½ cup milk and dip the bread in this mixture. (Use what's left over in scrambled eggs.) Melt 2 tablespoons of butter in a pan and sauté the bread in this over low heat until golden brown on both sides. Serve with maple cream or syrup, ginger marmalade, or cloudy honey.

CHEESE DISHES

CHEESE is not only good but nourishing and filling, and it can be used in many ways as a substitute for meat. Fresh cheese in its natural form is best for sandwiches, or to eat with crackers, or even by itself. The varieties on the market are numerous; for cooking the best kind is still American or "rat trap." This will grate better than any processed cheese and should be slightly stale to grate easily. Half a pound will probably be as much as you will want to buy at one time. Processed cheese will do for any dish that does not require grated cheese; it will melt easily if cut into small pieces, but you must choose a sharp variety as the flavor is blander than in regular cheese. Leftover bits of cheese can be used grated on soup or to top many baked dishes—cut in small cubes and pulverize in blender. If you have no cheese on hand, you can use fine crumbs made from cheese crackers as a baked crust. Always cook cheese over slow heat, either in the top of a double boiler if melting or in a slow oven if baking, since too much heat tends to toughen it.

Cheese Soufflé

　½　tablespoon butter
　½　tablespoon flour
　¼　cup milk
　¼　cup grated American cheese
　¼　teaspoon salt
　⅛　teaspoon dry mustard
　　　dash of paprika
　1　egg, separated

Melt the butter, blend in the flour, add the milk gradually, and cook for 5 minutes, stirring until mixture thickens. Add the cheese and seasonings, stir until melted, and remove from heat. Gradually stir in the egg yolk, well beaten, and then fold in the white, stiffly beaten. Put in a greased dish (a 6-inch size to allow for expansion while cooking) and set in a pan of hot water. Bake in a 350° F. oven for 35 to 40 minutes, until puffed and brown on top.

An excellent cheese soufflé is available frozen, but it may be too large for an individual serving. Allow to thaw, about 45 minutes. Cut in half, put one half in a small square baking dish, and re-freeze the other half. Allow less time to cook than the package directions, about 50 minutes.

Scalloped Cheese

3 slices white bread
½ cup grated or diced cheese
1 egg
½ cup milk
  salt and pepper
  pinch of dry mustard

Remove the crusts from the bread and cut the slices in small squares. Put them in a greased baking dish, mixing the cheese with the bread. Beat the egg with the milk and mix in the seasonings. Pour over the bread and cheese. Bake in a 350° F. oven for 20 minutes.

Welsh Rabbit

½ cup thin white sauce (p. 141)
¼ pound grated American cheese
⅛ teaspoon dry mustard
2 slices hot buttered toast

Add the cheese and mustard to the sauce, and heat over boiling water in a double boiler, stirring constantly until cheese is melted and mixture is smooth. Serve at once on toast.

This can be varied by adding ½ can condensed tomato soup or by using the cheese rabbit as a sauce over sardines which have been arranged on the toast and heated under the broiler for 2 or 3 minutes.

Tomato Cheese

    1 small onion
    1 tablespoon chopped green pepper
    1 tablespoon butter
    ½ can condensed tomato soup
       an equal amount of milk
    ¼ pound American cheese
    ¼ teaspoon Worcestershire sauce
       salt and pepper
    1 egg, slightly beaten

Mince the onion and cook with the green pepper in melted butter for 10 minutes over slow heat. Add the soup, diluted with the milk, and simmer for 5 minutes. Cut the cheese into small pieces, add to the soup, and put in the Worcestershire sauce. Cook slowly until cheese is all melted, stirring constantly, and then add salt, pepper, and the egg. Stir hard for a full minute, remove from fire, and serve immediately on toast, toasted English muffins, or on toasted crackers in a soup bowl. This is very filling, but very good.

Cheese Dreams

This generally means an open-face cheese sandwich toasted until the cheese is melted. An improvement is to spread a slice of rye or whole wheat bread with chutney, cover with a slice of American cheese, and top with two strips of bacon. Place under the broiler until the cheese begins to melt and the bacon is lightly browned. Be careful not to let the cheese come to the edge of the bread, as it will spread—and drip—when melted. A piece of foil underneath will help.

Cheese Muffin

Lightly toast an English muffin. Put a slice of cheese on each half, trimming the edges so that the cheese just fits. Put under the broiler until the cheese is bubbly. Sprinkle with dried dill or crumbled cooked bacon.

Spiedini

Lightly toast 3 slices Italian or French bread cut ½ inch thick. Put a slice of cheese, preferably Mozzarella, and 2 flat anchovy fillets on one piece of toast; top with another piece of toast, a cheese slice, and 2 more anchovy fillets; then cover with the third piece of toast. Secure this three-decker sandwich with two small skewers. Put in a greased baking dish, dot liberally with butter, and bake in a 400° F. oven until cheese is melted.

Cheese Spoonbread

Heat ½ cup milk in a double boiler. When hot add slowly ¼ cup corn meal (white or yellow). Stir constantly until the mixture is thickened and smooth. Remove from heat. Add a dash of salt, 1 tablespoon butter, a scant ½ cup shredded American cheddar cheese and 1 beaten egg yolk. Mix well. Beat 1 egg white until stiff and fold carefully into the corn meal mixture. Bake in a well-greased dish at 375° F. for 30 minutes and serve at once with warm honey butter: heat together over hot water 1 tablespoon butter and 2 tablespoons honey; when butter is melted mix well.

7

❦

PASTA AND
PANCAKES

PASTAS

MACARONI, noodles, and spaghetti are all cooked in the same way and are more or less interchangeable. Macaroni is the largest of the round varieties of *pasta,* the convenient Italian name for the whole group. It comes in "elbow" form as well as in long pieces. Spaghetti is the medium size and vermicelli the smallest, usually reserved for soup only. Noodles are flat. All combine well with cheese, tomatoes, and meat. They must be served piping hot, on hot plates, as they tend to cool off very quickly. Ravioli is little meat balls encased in a macaroni dough and served with tomato sauce. It is too complicated to make for one person but can be bought in cans. Serve very hot with plenty of grated Parmesan cheese.

General rules for cooking: macaroni and spaghetti double in bulk on cooking. Allow about 1 to 1⅓ ounces per portion. Use plenty of rapidly boiling salted water, about 4 cups of water to ½ cup uncooked macaroni. Add 1 teaspoon olive oil to cooking water so that pieces will not stick together when drained. Boil 9 to 12 minutes until tender but not mushy. Drain and rinse in cold running water to remove starch. Reheat with butter or sauce and keep hot until ready to serve.

Leftovers: add to minestrone or other clear soups.

Macaroni and Cheese

1 cup macaroni
¼ pound American cheese
   salt and pepper
1 tablespoon butter
½ cup thin white sauce (p. 141)

Cook the macaroni according to the general directions. Drain and rinse under running warm water. In a greased casserole put half the macaroni and half the cheese, either grated or diced, salt and pepper lightly, and dot with butter. Repeat with the rest of the macaroni, cheese, salt, pepper, and butter. Pour the sauce over the whole mixture and bake in a 400° F. oven 30 minutes, or until the top is golden brown.

Baked Spaghetti

1 small onion, minced
3 or 4 mushrooms, sliced
1 tablespoon butter or olive oil
¼ pound chopped meat
½ can condensed tomato soup or the same amount of tomato sauce
1½ cups cooked spaghetti
¼ cup grated cheese

Sauté the onion and mushroom in the butter or oil for about 10 minutes. Add the meat, break up with a fork, and fry until brown. Add the tomato soup or sauce, season if necessary, and bring to a boil. Mix this with the cooked spaghetti, put in a greased casserole, and top with grated cheese. Bake in a 375° F. oven for 10 or 15 minutes, until top is browned.

Italian Spaghetti

While the spaghetti is cooking—about 2 cups per serving—make the sauce. Mince 1 clove of garlic; add to 1 tablespoon olive oil, and fry lightly for 5 minutes until brown. Add ½ cup condensed tomato soup or prepared tomato sauce, salt, pepper, and a pinch of dried basil, and cook gently for 5 minutes. Keep hot until the spaghetti is ready. Put the spaghetti on a hot plate, pour the sauce on top, and add lots of grated Parmesan cheese. Chopped mushrooms or chicken livers, or both, sautéed in a little butter, can be added. Place them on top of the sauce before adding the cheese. Meat and clam sauces are available in small cans.

Spaghetti Carbonara

Cut 4 strips bacon into 1-inch pieces and sauté with 1 teaspoon butter until crisp. Cook ½ pound spaghetti according to package directions, drain, and return to pot. Beat 2 eggs until well mixed, then beat in ⅓ cup grated Parmesan or Romano cheese and a dash of black pepper. Pour the bacon and all fat in the pan over the spaghetti and mix well. Then pour over the egg and cheese mixture and mix further. Serve at once. Serves 2.

Pasta Sauces

Butter and grated cheese is the easiest. In addition to canned tomato, meat, and clam sauces, you might try sautéed chicken livers and mushrooms, separately or together; anchovies heated in butter with a dash of instant garlic; tuna fish broken up and combined with sliced black olives and added to tomato sauce.

Clam Sauce

To a 10½-ounce can white clam sauce add 2 tablespoons olive oil, 1 teaspoon instant garlic, and salt to taste. Simmer until very hot.

Baked Noodles

Cook noodles according to package directions in salted water. Rinse in cold water. Put a third of the noodles in a baking dish with a thin layer of dried bread crumbs and dot with butter.

Repeat to fill dish, making 3 layers in all. Add ½ cup cream, ending with crumbs and butter on top. Bake in 350° F. oven until sufficiently hot.

Noodles Romanoff

Cook ½ pound noodles according to package directions. Drain. Mix with 1 cup cottage cheese, 1 cup sour cream, 2 tablespoons minced onion, 1 teaspoon Worcestershire sauce, ½ teaspoon salt, and a dash each of Tabasco and garlic salt. Put in a buttered baking dish and bake 30 minutes in a 350° F. oven. Take out and cover the top with grated Parmesan or Romano cheese. Reheat until cheese is melted. Serves 3 or 4 but will keep well, covered, in refrigerator.

Chicken and Noodles

Cook ½ pound noodles according to package directions. Combine in a saucepan with ½ cup leftover chicken or boned canned chicken and ½ cup cooked peas, either fresh or canned. Add 1 tablespoon butter and plenty of seasoning—salt, pepper, onion salt, and celery salt. Or you could combine with cream sauce, top with buttered crumbs, and heat in oven. Serves 3 or 4.

Noodles and Mushrooms

A good way to use leftover noodles. Slice as many mushrooms as you want and sauté in butter over high heat for 5 minutes. Season with salt, pepper, and chopped parsley. Put cooked noodles in a greased baking dish and arrange with the mushrooms in layers. Top with bread crumbs, dot with butter, and heat in a 350° F. oven for about 10 minutes.

Noodles with Broccoli and Cottage Cheese

Combine ½ cup cottage cheese, ½ cup sour cream, 1 cup cooked chopped broccoli, 6 to 8 chopped scallions, and 2 tablespoons

white wine. Season lightly with salt, pepper, and nutmeg. Cook
½ pound noodles and put in a buttered baking dish. Pour the
cheese and broccoli mixture over the noodles. Sprinkle with
grated Parmesan cheese and dot with butter. Bake 30 minutes at
350° F. Serves 2.

PANCAKES

Basic Pancake Recipe

  1 cup all-purpose flour
1½ teaspoons baking powder
 ½ teaspoon salt
  1 egg, well beaten
 ¾ cup milk
  1 tablespoon salad oil

Sift together flour, baking powder, and salt. Beat egg and milk
together and add to flour mixture until smooth. Add the oil and
mix well. Heat a heavy skillet and grease lightly, then pour on the
pancake mixture to make 3 or 4 cakes. Brown over medium heat
until bubbles show, then turn and brown the other side. This
mixture makes about 6 cakes and could be doubled and the
leftover amount frozen. About ¼ cup blueberries can be added
as desired.

Cheese Pancakes

To preceding recipe add ½ cup grated sharp cheese, Cheddar or
Parmesan, and keep the batter a little thinner, using about 1
tablespoon less flour and 1 tablespoon more milk. Cook as directed, and remove from pan. Spread each pancake with cheese

sauce (p. 141). Roll up, put in shallow greased baking dish, and cover with more sauce. Bake until brown and bubbling.

Variation: Instead of cheese filling substitute 1 tablespoon minced sautéed mushrooms or cooked minced meat to which some grated cheese has been added.

Cottage Cheese Pancakes

     2 eggs
     ½ cup sieved cottage cheese
     ¾ cup sour cream
     ¾ cup flour
     ½ teaspoon baking soda
     1 teaspoon salt
        blueberries and sugar, or cinnamon sugar

Beat eggs well and mix with cheese. Add cream. Sift flour with soda and salt, add to egg mixture, and beat thoroughly. Let stand 5 minutes. Cook on hot greased griddle and serve with blueberries and sugar or cinnamon sugar.

Dessert Pancakes

Follow the basic pancake recipe on p. 61, adding 1 tablespoon sugar to batter. While the pancakes are cooking, heat currant jelly or any preferred jam in a double boiler, just enough to warm, not melt. Spread this on the cooked pancakes, roll up, and dust with powdered sugar.

8

---·⊛·---

RICE AND OTHER CEREALS

RICE DISHES

RICE, one of the most useful and versatile of cereal foods, lends itself to all kinds of combinations. It must be well cooked to begin with, dry and fluffy and never soggy. Minute rice takes about 10 minutes; follow directions on package. Regular rice will expand about four times the quantity when cooked; that is, ¼ cup raw rice will make 1 cup cooked. Minute rice expands about three times.

To cook white rice: Allow 3 tablespoons uncooked rice for one serving and cook in 2½ cups salted water. When the water is boiling furiously add the rice gradually and allow to cook for 15 to 18 minutes. Shake the pot gently once or twice while the rice is cooking so that it will not stick to the bottom, but do not stir. When the grains are tender, drain, rinse under running cold water through a sieve, and keep covered in the sieve over a little steaming hot water until ready to use.

To cook brown rice: Use the same amount of rice but only 1 cup of water. Cook in a double boiler 40 to 60 minutes, and do not rinse.

Wild rice is very good, very expensive, and not always obtainable; better save it for parties.

Freshly cooked rice goes well with any meat, particularly if there is plenty of gravy. Leftover rice is so easy to use, either as the basis of a new dish or as one ingredient, that at least two portions might as well be cooked at the same time. Leftover uses include clear soup, kedgeree, stuffed peppers, any meat or vegetable casserole, and desserts such as rice pudding and rice cream. Rice is essential with curries, and also can accompany creamed eggs, fish, chicken, or mushrooms.

Raisin Rice

For each cup of cooked rice, allow 1 tablespoon raisins. Put them in a strainer and steam over hot water until soft and plump. Combine with the rice and serve with curry, pork or veal chops, or hot tongue.

Baked Rice and Cheese

few drops of Worcestershire sauce
pinch of thyme
½ cup medium white sauce (p. 141)
½ cup cooked rice
¼ cup grated American cheese
buttered crumbs

Add the Worcestershire and thyme to the sauce. Arrange half the rice in a greased casserole and cover with half the sauce and half the cheese. Repeat, and top with the crumbs. Bake in a 350° F. oven for 15 minutes, or until cheese is melted.

Spanish Rice

1 medium-size tomato, sliced thin
2 or 3 mushrooms, chopped
1 tablespoon chopped green pepper
1 tablespoon onion flakes or chopped onion
salt and pepper
pinch of basil

½ cup cold water
½ to 1 cup cooked rice

Put all the ingredients except rice in a frying pan. Bring to a boil, reduce heat to low, cover, and simmer until vegetables are soft, about 20 minutes. Mix with cooked rice and reheat.

Rice Supreme

1 cup cooked rice
2 tablespoons milk
2 tablespoons butter
¼ teaspoon curry powder
1 tomato, sliced
¼ teaspoon salt
⅛ to ¼ pound cheese, sliced thin
¼ cup cream
2 slices bacon

If the rice is cold, reheat in the top of a double boiler with the milk to moisten it, then place in a greased casserole, pressing it flat. Melt the butter in a frying pan; add the curry powder, to-mato slices, and salt. Fry the tomato quickly, place on the rice, and top with the cheese. Pour the cream over all and bake in a 400° F. oven until the cheese is melted, about 10 minutes. Fry the bacon lightly, and put it on top of the casserole for the last 5 minutes.

Risotto with Mushrooms

3 tablespoons butter
1 small onion, minced
½ cup uncooked rice
salt and pepper
1 cup chicken bouillon
¼ pound mushrooms
¼ to ½ cup grated Parmesan cheese

Melt 1 tablespoon butter in a frying pan and brown the onion lightly in it. Add the raw rice and fry for 10 minutes, stirring to keep it from sticking to the pan. Season, add half the bouillon, simmer for 15 minutes, then add the rest of the bouillon and cook for 15 minutes more. All the liquid will be absorbed. While this is cooking, sauté the mushroom caps in 1 tablespoon butter. Add these and the third tablespoon of butter to the rice just before it is finished. Sprinkle all the cheese on top and serve.

OTHER CEREAL DISHES

Most people are used to the pattern of meat, potatoes, and a vegetable for the main course of their principal meal. If you choose to follow this general idea, remember that in place of potatoes you can serve rice or pasta with butter or gravy. Other potato substitutes are hominy grits, either plain with lots of butter, or fried, or baked. Fried corn-meal mush or farina does equally well. Spoonbread is easy to make and is very good.

To cook hominy grits, corn meal, and farina follow the general rules on the box, reducing the amount according to what you want. To fry, pack the cold cooked cereal in a baking pan rinsed with cold water. Cover and allow to get firm and cold. Cut in slices and sauté in butter or bacon fat until brown and crisp on both sides. Some people like maple syrup with this.

Baked Hominy Grits

   1 cup hot hominy grits
  ½ cup hot milk
   1 egg, slightly beaten
   1 tablespoon butter
     salt and pepper

Combine and put in a greased dish. Bake in a 350° F. oven 30 minutes, or until browned.

Spoonbread

1 cup milk
½ teaspoon salt
½ cup white corn meal
1 teaspoon baking powder
1 egg, separated

Scald milk in top of double boiler and add salt. Stir in corn meal gradually and cook over hot water until thick. Keep stirring until smooth, then remove from heat. Cool slightly. Add baking powder and egg yolk, well beaten. Fold in stiffly beaten egg white and pour into greased baking dish. Bake for about 30 minutes at 350° F. and serve at once.

Gnocchi

¾ cup milk
¼ cup farina or Cream of Wheat
   salt
½ tablespoon butter
½ cup grated cheese (preferably Parmesan)
½ egg (beat 1 egg lightly and use half)
½ tablespoon Worcestershire sauce

Heat the milk until almost boiling, add the farina or Cream of Wheat, and simmer 10 minutes. Add salt, butter, and ¼ cup of cheese, stirring until mixed thoroughly. Simmer 5 minutes and add the egg and Worcestershire sauce. Remove from the heat and spread out ½ to ¾ inch thick on a plate. Let it get cold, then cut into squares and put in a shallow greased baking dish. Dot with butter and sprinkle liberally with the rest of the cheese. Bake in a 400° F. oven about 15 minutes, until brown.

Polenta

In a heavy saucepan bring 1 cup milk to a boil. Stir in ¼ cup corn meal and cook for about 15 minutes, stirring constantly so that it does not stick to the bottom of the pan. Remove from heat and add 1 tablespoon butter, 2 tablespoons grated cheese, and ¼ teaspoon salt. When well mixed, pour into a greased baking dish and let cool. Top generously with more cheese, dot with butter, and bake at 425° F. for about 20 minutes, until cheese is melted and the top lightly browned. Serve with cooked sausages or crisp bacon. Serves 2.

Kasha

For this recipe use coarse groats, not fine or whole. Mix 1 cup groats with 1 beaten egg and 1 teaspoon salt. Melt 4 tablespoons butter in skillet. Add the groats and egg, stir, and cook gently until golden and quite dry. Pour 2 cups chicken or beef broth into the pan, cover, and simmer 15 to 20 minutes. The groats should be tender but not mushy, and the liquid absorbed. Add a generous amount of sweet butter to serve. Serves 4, but will keep.

Kasha Casserole

Melt 1 tablespoon butter in skillet and add ⅓ cup sliced mushrooms. Brown gently, stirring frequently. Put them in a greased baking dish. Add another tablespoon butter to skillet, and when melted stir in ½ cup buckwheat groats and sauté over low heat for 10 minutes. Add 1 tablespoon instant minced onion, salt, pepper, and 1¼ cups chicken broth. Cover and cook for 20 minutes, stirring frequently. If the kasha gets dry add more broth. Add the kasha to the mushrooms. Cover and bake in a 350° F. oven until the kasha is fluffy but still moist. Makes 1 generous or 2 medium servings.

9

————————❧————————

FISH AND SEAFOOD

FISH

THE IMPORTANT THING about fresh fish is that it must be *very* fresh and should be cooked on the same day on which it is bought. If fresh fish is not readily available in your locality for geographical reasons it can be obtained frozen, dried, canned, salted, or smoked. In buying fish this way one is as usual at the mercy of the packager; and the smallest can or package—with the possible exception of sardines—is enough for two servings. With fresh fish you can buy as little—or as much—as you can eat. For whole fish such as smelts, buy ¾ to 1 pound for one serving; for fillets or steaks ½ pound is generally enough; for solid pieces, cleaned and scaled, ½ pound.

Pan fish are little fish that are cooked whole in a frying pan. To prepare, roll in seasoned flour and fry in enough melted fat to cover the bottom of the pan. They are done as soon as they are brown—about 8 minutes over moderate heat. Serve with tartar sauce.

Steaks are generally broiled or baked, but can be fried when small, and this is the easiest way to cook them. Put the steak in hot fat—just below smoking—and allow to brown on one side; turn carefully and brown the other side. Remember that fish cooks very quickly. Serve steaks with lemon, butter, and chopped parsley.

Fillets are cooked the same way but, being thinner than steaks, they cook even faster, and must be turned very carefully so as not to break. They can also be baked in a shallow greased baking dish. Dot well with butter and season. Bake in 400° F. oven for 10 minutes or a little longer, depending on the thickness of the fish.

Pieces cut from a large fish such as salmon or halibut are generally boiled, served whole with a sauce, or flaked and reheated in sauce. To cook, tie the fish in cheesecloth, place it in enough cold water to cover it, and add 1 teaspoon salt and 1 teaspoon vinegar. Bring to a boil, reduce the heat, cover, and simmer for 5 minutes for 1 pound or less. As boiled fish lends itself to being used in several ways, it is a good idea to get enough for two servings and use it in a different way the second time.

Baked Fish Fillets I

Put the fish in a greased baking dish. Combine 1 tablespoon butter, juice of ½ lemon, salt, pepper, a pinch of dried salad herbs, and parsley and spread on fish. Pour in about ¼ cup dry white wine, to cover the bottom of the dish but not the fish. Sprinkle with paprika and slivered almonds. Bake 15 minutes in a 475° F. oven.

Baked Fish Fillets II

- 3 tablespoons butter
- 3 scallions, chopped
- 2 fish fillets
- salt and pepper
- ¼ teaspoon curry powder
- ¼ cup white wine
- 1 tablespoon flour
- ¼ cup milk
- 1 tomato, sliced
- ¼ cup mushroom caps
- 1 pimiento

Melt 2 tablespoons butter, add the scallions, and cook very slowly for 5 minutes. Add the fish, seasonings, and wine. Poach gently for 10 minutes. Put the fish in a baking dish. Reserve the liquid. Melt 1 tablespoon butter, blend in flour, add milk, and cook until thickened. Add half the reserved liquid gradually. Pour over the fish. Put the tomato, mushrooms, and pimiento on top of the fish. Season lightly with more salt and pepper. Pour the remaining liquid over all. Bake 20 minutes in a 350° F. oven. Serves 2 liberally.

Baked Fish Steaks—Halibut, Salmon, Swordfish

Buy a steak weighing about ½ pound. Put it in a shallow greased baking dish and cover with this sauce: melt 2 tablespoons butter; add 1 squeeze fresh lemon juice, ¼ teaspoon vinegar, ¼ teaspoon Worcestershire sauce, salt, and pepper. Mix well and pour over fish. Preheat oven to 450° F. Bake 25 to 30 minutes, depending on thickness of the fish. A little dry white wine can be added for the last 10 minutes.

Codfish Cakes

Codfish cakes can be bought ready to fry, either canned or frozen. Shape into patties, dredge with flour and fry in hot bacon fat until brown on both sides. Serve plain or with bacon.

Flounder and Zucchini

Cut one medium-size zucchini into ⅛-inch slices, leaving the skin on. Cook in 1 tablespoon melted butter with a pinch each of dried rosemary, basil, and parsley, until soft on both sides (about 10 minutes). Put a seasoned fish fillet in a shallow greased baking dish, cover with the cooked zucchini, and top with bread crumbs and another tablespoon of melted butter. Cook uncovered in a 350° F. oven until fish is tender, about 10 minutes. Add a sprinkling of lemon juice when serving.

Fillet of Flounder

Follow general directions for panned fish (see p. 69); or put in a shallow baking dish with a few chopped mushrooms, cover with thin cream sauce (p. 141), and bake for 10 minutes. Then place under the broiler to brown the sauce lightly.

Baked Fillet of Flounder

Put 1 or 2 fillets of flounder (depending on size) in a shallow baking dish with a small white onion, sliced, and a can of button mushrooms. Sprinkle liberally with lemon juice and dot with butter. Season with salt, pepper, thyme, and crumbled bay leaf; add ¼ cup dry white wine. Cover the dish with aluminum foil, sealing the edges tightly. Bake for 15 minutes in a 350° F. oven. Remove foil carefully so as not to burn your hands with steam.

Variation: Use 4 chopped scallions and dry vermouth instead of onions and wine.

Sole with Mushrooms and Cheese

In a skillet make a court bouillon of liquid from a 2-ounce can of sliced mushrooms, some dried vegetable flakes, a little water, and dry white wine—enough to cover the skillet about ½ inch deep. Heat just to boiling. Poach the fish in this bouillon 5 to 8 minutes, simmering gently until it just flakes. Remove carefully to a shallow baking dish and cover with the sliced mushrooms. Make a sauce of ½ can condensed cream of mushroom or chicken soup, thinned slightly with dry white wine, and 1 tablespoon grated Parmesan cheese. (The dish can be made ahead up to this point.) When ready to heat sprinkle with more cheese. Bake about 10 minutes at 375° F. until sauce is bubbling.

Salmon

Use fresh, boiled, or canned salmon. Serve with cream sauce (p. 141), ½ pound of fish to 1 cup sauce, or cream and bake with bread crumbs. Serve cold in one piece with mayonnaise, or flaked in salad with chopped celery. This may also be used for stuffing a chilled tomato or in sandwiches.

Kedgeree

>   1 tablespoon butter
>   1 very small onion, minced
>   1 teaspoon curry powder
>   salt and pepper
>   ½ cup flaked cooked salmon
>   ½ cup cooked rice
>   1 hard-boiled egg, chopped
>   ½ cup light cream

Melt the butter in a saucepan, add onion, and cook slowly until golden yellow, about 10 minutes. Stir in curry powder and seasonings, add rest of ingredients, mix well, and heat thoroughly.

Sardines

Sardines come in very small cans if desired. Choose the largest sardines, however, no matter what the size of the can. They may be used cold in salads and sandwiches and are also excellent when heated and served on toast. Simply heat in a frying pan in their own oil until hot—they do not have to be browned. The skin and bones can be removed either before or after cooking.

Broiled Sardines I

>   2 slices of bread
>   1 small can sardines
>   1 tablespoon lemon juice
>   pinch of dry mustard
>   few drops of Worcestershire sauce

Toast one side of the bread. Put the sardines on the untoasted side. Mix the seasonings with the oil in the can, spread on the sardines, and broil until well heated.

Broiled Sardines II

Drain the contents of a small can of sardines and split sardines in half lengthwise, removing bones, if any. Toast 1 or 2 slices white bread. Put the sardines on the bread, cover with a dash of chili sauce, and top with grated sharp cheese. Broil until the cheese melts. Serve garnished with lemon slices and a little grated raw onion.

Sardines on Muffins

Drain the oil from a small can of sardines, reserving 1 tablespoon. Sprinkle the fish, still in the can, with fresh minced parsley and put the can in the oven to warm at lowest heat. Toast 2 English muffin halves. Make this sauce: warm ¼ cup sour cream over lowest heat; add the sardine oil and 1 teaspoon butter; gently heat to melting; stir in ¼ teaspoon dry mustard, 1 teaspoon lemon juice, salt, and cayenne pepper. Spread the sardines on the muffins, cover with the sauce, and sprinkle with chopped hard-boiled egg.

Shad Roe

If it is fresh, parboil first so that it will keep its shape. Put the roe into boiling water with 1 teaspoon salt and 1 teaspoon vinegar. Reduce the heat and simmer for 15 minutes. Take out of the water, dredge lightly with flour, and fry in bacon fat over moderate heat until brown on both sides, about 20 minutes. If canned, parboiling is not necessary. Serve plain or with bacon.

Tuna à la King

Melt 2 tablespoons butter over low heat. Add 2 tablespoons chopped green pepper and sauté for 5 minutes. Stir in ¼ pound fresh mushrooms (caps and stems), sliced, or an 8-ounce can of sliced mushrooms. Sauté 10 minutes or until the pepper is soft. Remove to the top of a double boiler, retaining about 1 tablespoon of melted butter in the skillet. To this add 1 tablespoon flour; blend thoroughly. Add very gradually 1 cup milk, stirring constantly to avoid lumps. As sauce thickens season with salt, pepper, and cayenne. Combine 1 can tuna, well drained and flaked, and 1 tablespoon sliced canned pimiento with the mushrooms and peppers; pour the sauce over all. Heat over hot water, and just before serving add 2 tablespoons sherry. Serve on white rice or toast.

Tuna Casserole (or Pie)

Combine ½ can tuna chunks with 1 hard-boiled egg, cut in quarters. A few cooked peas can be added if available. Put in an individual baking dish, cover with ⅓ can Cheddar cheese soup (undiluted), and top with buttered crumbs or crumbled potato chips. Bake 10 to 15 minutes in a 350° F. oven until sauce is bubbling and crumbs are brown.

For a pie, use carrots as well as peas, or some diced cooked potato. Put in a shallow dish and cover with pie crust. Cook for 10 to 15 minutes in a 350° F. oven until crust browns.

Creamed Tuna

Drain the oil from a 3¼ oz. can of tuna into a small skillet. Stir in 1 teaspoon or a little more flour and mix until all the flour is absorbed. Gradually add enough milk to make a good thick sauce. Season to taste. Add the fish, in chunks. Then add 3 or 4 chopped scallions, including green parts, 1 tablespoon chopped green pepper, a few sliced stuffed olives, and about 1 cup leftover cooked pasta, any size or shape. Cover and cook over moderate heat 5 minutes. The trick is making the sauce with tuna oil.

Tuna and Crab Meat

Use in the same way as salmon, either in cream sauce, creamed and baked with bread crumbs, in salads, or in sandwiches. Tuna combines well with mushrooms. Combine crab meat with artichoke hearts.

Fish Puff

Use any leftover cooked fish or canned tuna. Flake and season with 1 tablespoon minced onion, 1 tablespoon minced parsley, and a dash of pepper. Combine with an equal amount of mashed potatoes. Add 1 egg, lightly beaten, and 1 tablespoon butter or margarine. Test for seasoning. Put in a greased baking dish and bake at 450° F. about 15 minutes, or until brown.

SHELLFISH

Soft-Shell Crabs

Buy 2 small or 1 large crab. Season with salt and pepper and fry about 7 minutes in plenty of butter, turning once. Serve with tartar sauce.

Boiled Lobster

Unless your market sells lobsters already boiled, be sure the lobster is alive when you buy it. Buy one weighing 1 to 2 pounds, unless you want leftover meat. Plunge the live lobster immediately into enough boiling salted water to cover it. Boil briskly for 15 to 25 minutes, depending on size—15 minutes for 1 pound, 20 for 1½ pounds, 25 for 2 pounds. Let it cool somewhat before splitting from end to end on the under side with a sharp knife. Remove the small sack near the head, but leave in the green fat and red coral, which are quite edible. The tail will come out in one piece, but the claws will have to be cracked and the meat picked out. Eat hot with lots of melted butter or cold with mayonnaise. Leftover meat can be used in the same ways as tuna or crab meat.

Rock Lobster Tails

These come frozen, generally 2 to a package. Boil both, according to directions on the package. Serve one hot with melted butter and lemon juice. Use the other one the next day, either in Newburg sauce or cold with mayonnaise flavored with lemon juice and tarragon.

Broiled Scallops

One-half pound is ample for one person. If very large, cut the scallops into pieces before cooking. Wipe each scallop with a damp cloth. Dip in melted butter and then in bread crumbs. Put under the broiler in a shallow pan that has ½ inch melted fat in the bottom, and broil under a hot flame for 10 minutes, turning occasionally until brown all over. Season with salt and pepper and serve with tartar sauce.

Herbed Broiled Scallops

½   pound bay scallops
     salt and pepper
¼   teaspoon dried basil
¼   teaspoon dried rosemary
½   lemon, thinly sliced
     dash of Tabasco
 2   tablespoons salad oil

Place all ingredients in a bowl, stir, and cover. Refrigerate 2 hours or longer. Then remove the scallops from the marinade and arrange in one layer in a baking dish. Broil about 3 minutes, then turn and broil 3 minutes longer. Do not overcook—the scallops will get tough.

Baked Scallops

Preheat oven to 450° F. Grease a shallow casserole or shirred egg dish and spread the scallops in one layer. Season with salt and pepper. Add 2 tablespoons cream and sprinkle with 2 table-spoons bread crumbs. Dot with butter and bake for 15 minutes. Serve at once.

Shrimps

Fresh shrimps are a lot of trouble to prepare, but they can be bought ready to eat in cans. Be sure to rinse very thoroughly before using. Serve shrimps heated in a curry sauce with rice, or baked in a casserole with cooked cauliflower, cream sauce, and grated cheese. Cold shrimps, chopped and mixed with chopped celery, can be used for salads and sandwiches. Frozen shrimps are usually ready to cook.

Shrimp Creole

1 small white onion, diced
1 small green pepper, diced (½ cup)
1 tablespoon butter
1 can tomatoes (⅔ cup)
 salt and pepper
 chili powder
 Tabasco
 rosemary
½ cup cooked shrimps
 cooked rice

Sauté onion and pepper in the butter until soft. Add tomatoes and season with salt, pepper, chili powder, Tabasco, and rose-mary. Cover and simmer 10 minutes over low heat. Add shrimps; heat thoroughly. Serve on hot rice.

Shrimp with Egg and Celery

Combine as many shrimps as you want with ¼ to ⅓ cup cooked diced celery and 1 hard-boiled egg, diced. Mix with condensed cream of celery soup slightly thinned with water in which the celery was cooked. Heat in a double boiler and serve on toast.

Seafood en Coquille

Fill a small greased baking dish with a mixture of cooked or canned diced shrimp, lobster, or scallops, either alone or in combination, in a sauce of condensed cream of mushroom soup thinned with a little light cream and flavored with sherry. Sprinkle liberally with grated Parmesan cheese and dot with butter. Brown under the broiler and serve very hot.

Seafood Strata

Butter 1 slice firm white bread and put it, butter side up, in a greased individual square baking dish. Trim to fit if necessary. Combine flaked crab meat or chopped shrimp with finely chopped celery and minced onion, mixed with enough mayonnaise to soften. Heap this on the bread. Sprinkle shredded Swiss cheese on top. Cover with another slice of buttered bread, butter side down. In a mixing bowl beat 1 egg with ½ cup milk, ¼ teaspoon dry mustard, and a dash of black pepper. Pour this over the bread, cover, and let sit for 2 hours or longer. Bake 35 to 40 minutes in a 350° F. oven, until puffy and slightly brown. Let it cool a few minutes before serving.

Crab and Shrimp Newburg

Frozen Newburg—lobster, crab meat, or shrimps—is available but expensive, especially as there is generally much more sauce than seafood. One package is barely enough for 2 servings. Try this instead.

    1 teaspoon sherry
    ½ cup medium white sauce (p. 141)
    ½ cup crab meat
    ½ cup shrimps

Add sherry to the sauce when it is ready, pour over the crab meat and shrimps in a baking dish, and heat thoroughly in a 350° F. oven.

10

---

§

MEAT AND POULTRY

MEAT is generally considered the hardest menu problem when cooking for one, but actually there are as many variations of small-quantity meats as there are of fish or other protein dishes. The larger cuts must, of course, be reserved for meals when you have guests, and the leftovers from them can be used up in a number of interesting ways. Leftover slices are good for sandwiches and smaller bits for stews, curries, hash, and casseroles. Save the bones for soup.

---

§

BEEF

Club Steak

Season with salt and pepper and broil or pan-fry for 5 minutes on each side. Allow 1 small steak per serving.

Hamburg Steak

Season with salt and pepper, Worcestershire sauce, and onion salt or flakes. Fry 5 to 8 minutes on each side in bacon fat or broil in the oven. Allow ¼ pound per serving.

Another way to cook hamburgers is to roll the patties in very coarsely ground black pepper—the best flavor is obtained from fresh peppercorns broken with a hammer or pestle. Broil and, when ready, put in a pan with a little melted butter and 1 tablespoon dry vermouth for each patty. Baste and heat for a few minutes.

Cheeseburgers

Divide the usual-size hamburg patty in half and pat out to make two thin rounds. Put a slice of cheese between them and pinch the edges of the meat together so that no cheese shows. Broil as usual. Cheddar or Swiss cheese can be used, or Roquefort for a special flavor.

Meat Loaf

Put 3 heaping tablespoons seasoned bread crumbs in a baking dish; pour in enough dry red wine to moisten well. Mix in 1 egg and 2 teaspoons instant onion. Season with salt, pepper, oregano, and parsley. Add 1 pound ground chuck and mix thoroughly. Mold into a smooth round in the dish. Bake in a 400° F. oven for 20 minutes. Add ½ can mushroom gravy and bake 10 minutes more. Leftovers can be served cold, reheated, or frozen for future use.

Ground-Beef Stew

Cook 1 minced onion in bacon fat 10 minutes over low heat. Add ¼ pound chopped round steak and brown. Add ½ cup canned or stewed tomatoes, salt, and pepper, and simmer until the mixture is thick, about 30 minutes. Serve with rice or noodles. See page 169 for another version.

Dried Beef

Comes in small jars or ½-pound packages. Soak 15 minutes in cold water. Shred with your fingers and add about ½ cup meat to ½ cup medium white sauce (p. 141). Or add to scrambled eggs before cooking, ¼ cup dried beef to 2 eggs.

Corned Beef Hash

Buy any of the usual brands in cans. Heat 1½ to 2 cups of hash in a small frying pan with 1 tablespoon bacon fat and brown thoroughly. Serve plain, or with a poached egg or tomato sauce. One 15 oz. can makes three servings, so use leftovers as stuffing for green peppers or combine with finely chopped cooked beets to make **Red Flannel Hash**.

Frankfurters and Kidney Beans

Slice 2 or 3 frankfurters and sauté in melted butter with 1 tablespoon minced onion and 2 tablespoons each chopped celery and green pepper, until soft and brown. Add ½ cup canned tomato sauce or beef gravy and a small can of kidney beans, with juice. Season with salt and pepper and a dash of Worcestershire sauce. Cover and simmer 10 minutes.

Frankfurters and Peas

3 or 4 frankfurters
    1 teaspoon butter
       pinch of dry mustard
   ¼ teaspoon sugar
   ½ teaspoon chili sauce
   ⅓ cup cream
       salt and pepper
    1 cup small (French) canned peas

Boil the frankfurters until almost tender, about 10 minutes—test with a fork, which should pierce them easily. Peel and cut in 3 pieces. Make a sauce by melting the butter, add mustard and sugar, then chili sauce, cream, and a little salt and pepper. Cook the frankfurters in this sauce over low heat until thoroughly heated, and, to serve them, combine with the peas, which have been heated in another saucepan and drained. Serves 2.

LAMB

Chops

Allow 1 loin chop or 2 rib chops per serving. Broil rib chops about 10 minutes on each side, loin chops 12 to 15 minutes. An English chop, which is wrapped around a piece of kidney and is very good, should be broiled a little longer, as it is cut thicker. Serve chops with butter and salt and pepper.

Lamb Patties

These are cakes of ground lamb like hamburgers. Allow one per serving. Mix with a few onion flakes, bread crumbs, salt and pepper, and a pinch of dried marjoram—which does everything for the flavor—and fry in bacon fat 5 to 8 minutes on each side, or broil in the oven.

Lamb Stew

Sauté ½ pound lamb, cut in pieces and seasoned, in enough olive oil to cover the bottom of the pan, with 1 clove of garlic, chopped. When the lamb is brown on both sides, put it in a deep casserole and throw away the garlic. Cook in the saucepan 3 small carrots, sliced and scraped, and 2 medium white onions, peeled and whole, for a few minutes, but do not brown. Put these in the casserole with the lamb and 2 medium potatoes, peeled and cut in ½-inch slices. Mix well. Add ⅔ cup beef bouillon, ⅓ cup white wine, ⅛ teaspoon thyme, ¼ teaspoon marjoram, and 1 bay leaf. Cover tightly and simmer in a 375° F. oven for 1¼ hours, or use a pressure cooker. This makes enough for two meals, but like all stews improves on reheating. Any cooked leftover vegetables—except beets—can be added the second night.

Shepherd's Pie

Grind 1 cup cooked lamb, add 1 minced onion and 1 tablespoon butter, put in deep dish, cover with mashed potatoes, and bake at 375° F. until potatoes begin to brown.

PORK

Pork Chops

Allow 1 rib chop per serving. Brown quickly on both sides in melted bacon fat, reduce heat, add ¼ cup hot water, cover, and simmer slowly for 30 to 40 minutes until tender. Red wine can be substituted for the water. If the liquid is used up in cooking add a little more as necessary.

Pork Sausage

Allow ¼ pound per serving, either in links or sausage meat. Prick the links in several places with a fork before cooking so that they will not burst their skins while frying. Fry about 10 minutes over moderate heat, browning on both sides. Sausage will make its own grease as it cooks, so no extra fat is necessary.

Scrapple

Allow ¼ pound per serving. Cut in ½-inch slices, dredge with flour, and fry quickly in hot fat until brown and crisp on both sides. Turn carefully with a pancake lifter. Serve plain or with a poached or fried egg. Leftover scrapple can be baked in a deep dish with a mashed potato crust.

Boiled Ham

Allow ⅛ to ¼ pound thinly shaved boiled ham per serving. Melt ½ teaspoon currant jelly with 1 teaspoon butter, stir in the ham, and heat thoroughly.

Ham, Cheese, and Vegetable Casserole

- 1 small white onion, minced
- 1 tablespoon butter
- 1 tablespoon flour
- ½ cup milk
-    salt and pepper
- 1 cold boiled potato, diced
- 1 slice of ham, shredded or ground
- ½ small summer squash, diced and cooked
- ¼ cup grated cheese

Sauté the onion in the butter, blend in the flour, and add the milk to make a sauce. Season with salt and pepper. Put in a greased casserole the potato, ham, and squash. Pour the sauce on this and top with the cheese. Bake in a 350° F. oven about 20 minutes, or until the cheese is melted.

Ham and Asparagus in Cheese Sauce

Use fresh cooked, frozen or the best quality canned asparagus and allow 4 stalks per serving. Roll 2 stalks in a slice of thin boiled ham. Repeat with 2 more stalks. Put both rolls in an individual baking dish, cover with cheese sauce (p. 141) and bake about 20 minutes in a 350° F. oven until slightly browned.

Ham Steak in Madeira Sauce

Buy a small ham steak, ⅔ to ¾ pound, about ⅝ inch thick. Spread with prepared mustard and sprinkle with 1 tablespoon brown sugar. Put in a flat baking dish and add enough water to fill the dish without covering the ham, about ½ cup. Bake for 30 minutes at 375° F. Remove from the oven, sprinkle with 1 to 2 tablespoons flour, and blend this with the liquid. Simmer over low heat until the sauce thickens a little, then add 2 tablespoons Madeira.

Bacon

Buy ½ pound at a time. Fry until lightly brown on both sides— it will turn darker when removed from the pan. Drain well on 2 thicknesses of paper towel. Or use a special pan which drains off the grease. Serve with eggs, liver, tomatoes, mushrooms, fish cakes, or in sandwiches.

Canadian bacon has less fat and is more like ham. Fry as you would regular bacon, but be careful that it does not stick to the pan—it may be necessary to add a little extra grease. Serve with eggs, etc.; it is particularly good with spoonbread or baked hominy grits and with waffles or French toast and maple syrup.

Vienna Sausage and Mushroom Casserole

    4 scallions, chopped
    1 tablespoon chopped green pepper
   ¼ pound mushroom caps, chopped
    1 tablespoon butter
    1 cup cooked rice
   ¼ pound (or 8-ounce can) Vienna sausage
       salt and pepper
       pinch each of basil, marjoram, sage
    1 cup cooked or canned tomatoes

Sauté the scallions, pepper, and mushrooms in butter over low heat for 10 minutes. Put them in a greased casserole with the rice and sausage, cut in inch lengths. Season, and pour over this mixture the tomatoes with as little juice as possible. Mix together and bake in a 350° F. oven 15 minutes.

Vienna Sausage Casserole

A simpler version than the above. Combine 1 small can of sausage with 1½ cups cooked rice. Season with marjoram, parsley and instant onion. Add a can of condensed vegetable-beef soup and heat in a double boiler, not in the oven. (I invented this one evening when time and supplies were short and named it "Desperation Casserole.")

Vienna sausage and cooked rice or macaroni in cheese sauce can be endlessly combined with most cooked vegetables. If no stewed tomatoes are on hand use tomato or vegetable juice, and always include some form of onion. A quick **cassoulet** can be made with sausage and canned red kidney beans, using juice from both cans and flavoring with onion salt.

VEAL

Veal Chops

Allow 1 loin chop per serving. Cook the same way as pork chops (p. 84). Another way is to brown the chop 5 minutes on each side in bacon fat; season; reduce the heat, add ½ cup dry white wine, 2 tablespoons chopped ripe olives, and 1 teaspoon chopped fresh chives (or 1 tablespoon dried). Cover and simmer over very low heat for 45 minutes.

Veal Paprika

Buy 1 pound veal cut for stew. Sauté 1 sliced onion in 1 tablespoon butter until yellow. Add the meat and brown slightly. Stir in ½ tablespoon paprika. Use good Hungarian paprika—mild, not hot. Add enough chicken broth or white wine to cover the meat. Simmer, uncovered, until the meat is tender and most of the liquid has evaporated (about 1 hour). Add 1 cup sour cream and heat gently for about 10 minutes.

Minced Veal

Grind ½ cup leftover veal, combine with ½ cup thin white sauce (p. 141), and serve on toast.

Veal with Tarragon

Use veal cut for stew and pound well with a potato masher to tenderize. Braise in melted margarine or vegetable shortening until the pink color of the meat disappears. Season with salt, pepper and 1 teaspoon dried tarragon. Add ½ cup bouillon or chicken broth and ½ cup dry white wine. Cook 12 minutes in pressure cooker or 1½ to 2 hours on medium heat. Add a dash of Kitchen Bouquet before serving.

VARIETY MEATS

Sweetbreads

One pair makes 2 servings. Cover with 2 cups boiling water to which ½ teaspoon salt and 1 teaspoon vinegar have been added. Cover and simmer 15 minutes. Drain and chill in ice water. This should be done as soon as sweetbreads are brought home, as they do not keep well. The rest of the cooking can be done later. To cream, cut in small pieces and heat in 1 cup medium white sauce (p. 141). To broil, remove tubes and cords and cut lengthwise. Dip in melted butter and broil 6 to 8 minutes until browned.

Ox Tongue

May be bought, sliced, at the delicatessen. It does not keep well. Heat with raisin sauce (page 144), and serve on rice.

Lamb Kidneys

Allow 3 to 4 kidneys per serving. Wash, remove fat tubes and membrane, and cut into small pieces. Sauté 1 small minced onion in 1 tablespoon bacon fat, add the kidneys, and sauté 5 minutes. Stir in 1 tablespoon flour, blend, and add ¼ cup bouillon. Season with salt and pepper and simmer for 10 minutes, and just before removing from the fire add ½ tablespoon sherry.

Veal Kidney

Allow 1 whole kidney per serving. Although larger than lamb kidneys they are just as delicate and require less preparation. To sauté, follow directions for lamb kidneys above. They may also be baked, fat and all, in a 400° F. oven for 30 minutes. Rich but good.

Chicken Livers

Allow ¼ pound per serving. Dredge lightly with flour, salt, and pepper. Sauté whole in melted butter 5 to 8 minutes, until brown. Leftover chicken livers make a good spread. Put through the grinder, mix with mayonnaise, and season with onion salt and powdered marjoram. Chill before using.

Beef Liver

Calves' liver is preferable, although mature beef liver is quite edible. Allow 1 generous slice per serving, ¼ to ½ pound. Wipe the liver with a damp cloth, sprinkle with seasoned flour, and cook quickly in hot fat, turning once. It will be brown outside and still juicy inside in about 5 minutes.

CHICKEN

Broiled Chicken

Allow half of a small broiler (1½ to 2 pounds) per serving. Wipe with a damp cloth, then rub with vegetable oil, and sprinkle with salt and pepper. Use moderate heat (350° F.) on the broiler and keep the chicken 5 to 6 inches below the flame and in a pan to catch the drippings. Place skin side down until lightly browned, then turn and cook other side until brown. Baste with drippings and cook about 10 minutes more on both sides, about 30 to 40 minutes in all. Keep basting and do not allow the chicken to brown too fast. Serve with its own juice and more butter if necessary.

Chicken Fricassee

The remaining half of a chicken broiler or individual parts can be browned in melted butter and then stewed with about ½ inch of water in the pot. Add seasonings and some chopped onion and celery, cover, and simmer for 30 minutes until tender. Remove from the pot, thicken the gravy with a little flour, and serve with boiled rice.

Baked Chicken in Wine

Another way of cooking chicken parts is to brown the chicken on both sides in melted butter over medium heat. Transfer, with what butter remains, to a shallow baking dish. Pour over ¼ cup dry white wine, season with salt and pepper, and sprinkle with tarragon. Cover the dish with aluminum foil and seal the edges tightly. Bake in a 350° F. oven for 30 minutes. Remove the foil very carefully so as not to burn your hands with the steam.

Crisp Baked Chicken

Baking is a very easy method of cooking, as it requires hardly any attention. Put the chicken pieces in a roasting pan, flesh side up. Spread liberally with softened butter or margarine. Bake uncovered in a 350° F. oven for 1¼ to 1½ hours, basting occasionally. About halfway through, sprinkle with salt and a little pepper. When done, the pieces should be brown and crisp on top and the fat in the pan should provide enough gravy.

Chicken à la King

Leftover chicken can be creamed and combined with mushrooms, pimientos, and a dash of sherry to make chicken à la king.

Deviled Chicken Legs

With a sharp knife score a cooked drumstick with crisscross lines, about ½ inch apart. Spread all over with butter and dry mustard. Broil until sizzling hot on both sides.

Creamed Chicken on Corn Toasts

    1 tablespoon butter
    1 tablespoon flour
      salt
    ⅓ cup chicken broth
    2 heaping tablespoons sour cream
    ½ cup cooked diced chicken
    1 tablespoon bourbon or rye whiskey

Melt the butter in a double boiler, blend in the flour and salt, add the broth and allow to thicken. Stir in the sour cream and chicken and heat thoroughly. Just before serving add the whiskey. Serve on hot corn toasts. The contrast of the creamy chicken and the coarse corn bread is very pleasing. 2 servings.

Chicken Curry

Melt 1 tablespoon butter over low heat. Add 1 small white onion, sliced, and sauté 10 to 15 minutes, until onion is golden but not brown. Blend in 1 tablespoon flour, ¼ teaspoon curry powder, ⅛ teaspoon salt, and a dash of black pepper. Stir in gradually 1 cup chicken bouillon (1 cup hot water with 1 chicken bouillon cube dissolved in it). Add to the sauce ½ cup diced chicken.

Serve with boiled white rice and chutney. Chopped salted peanuts and raisins, shredded coconut, or cooked crumbled bacon may be sprinkled on top.

Variation: For chicken you may substitute any one of the following: ½ cup diced roast lamb; ½ cup diced roast veal; ½ cup cooked shrimp; or 2 hard-boiled eggs, sliced.

Rock Cornish Game Hen

These are really little individual roasting chickens. If bought frozen, allow to thaw 2 hours at room temperature or ½ hour in hot water (leave in its plastic bag). When ready, spread with soft butter. Season and stuff with 3 tablespoons seasoned bread crumbs mixed with just enough butter and water to moisten the crumbs. Place in a pan with a little water and roast 15 minutes at 450° F. and then 20 minutes at 350° F., basting frequently.

11

---⚛---

VEGETABLES

VEGETABLES offer the widest range of choice for single servings, for they can not only be bought in small quantities but can all be used in at least two ways, sometimes by simply changing the sauce. Recipes in this chapter are for one or two servings, with suggestions for leftovers, but as a general rule it will save time to cook at least two servings of the vegetable in the first place, saving half to use the next day in another way. Vegetables can be reheated, either in a little of their own juice over low heat or in a sieve over boiling water with a lid to keep the steam in, but it is certainly more interesting to try something besides merely reheating.

General rules for cooking vegetables:

- Do not prepare a long time ahead, as vitamins are lost in this way.
- Do not leave any vegetables soaking in water except broccoli, Brussels sprouts, cabbage, or cauliflower, which should be soaked in cold water for half an hour to remove any lurking insects.
- Always put the vegetable in boiling water and count the cooking time after the water starts to boil again.
- Add salt halfway through the cooking period, except when noted in the specific directions which follow. Use as little water as possible, usually about 2 cups to 1 cup of vegetables, but for members of the cabbage family use more water. Cook

over moderate heat. The cooking time for any vegetable will vary a little depending on the age and also the size of pieces into which it is cut.

- Drain well, as soon as cooked, saving the juice for soups, and serve with butter, salt, and pepper. Some vegetables combine well with cream sauce or hollandaise.

Frozen vegetables will save much preparation time and often cooking time as well. The usual package yields three portions. Vegetables such as broccoli, cauliflower, and Hubbard squash, too large for the single diner, are particularly convenient in frozen form.

Canned vegetables are less tasty than frozen or fresh. The most satisfactory ones are julienne-cut carrots and beets, kernel or cream-style corn, and tiny French peas, not at all like fresh peas but good in their own way. An 8-ounce can gives 2 portions.

BUYING AND COOKING TABLE

FOR ONE SERVING

Vegetable	Quantity	Boiling Time (minutes)	Ways of Using Up
Artichoke	1	30–40	hearts in salad
Asparagus	½ lb.	10–20	omelet, salad
Beans, green	¼ lb.	20–25	salad
Beans, lima	½ lb.	20–30	soup, succotash, salad
Corn	2 ears	6–10	soup, succotash
Mushrooms	¼ lb.	5–8	soup, omelet, casserole
Onions	¼ lb.*	20–30	see below
Peas	¼ lb.	10–20	soup, salad, creamed dishes
Peppers	1	5–10	
Potatoes, sweet	1	20–30	see below
Potatoes, white	1 or 2*	20–40	see below
Spinach	1 lb.	8–10	soup, with eggs
Summer squash	1 small	10–15	casserole
Tomatoes	1*	5–15	see below
Zucchini	1 or 2	10–12	baked

FOR TWO SERVINGS

Acorn squash	1		stuffed
Baked beans	1 can		with frankfurters
Beets	1 bunch	30–45	Harvard, hash
Beet greens		10–15	
Carrots	1 bunch	10–20	riced, glazed
Cauliflower	1 very small	10–20	creamed, with browned crumbs, au gratin
Celery	1 bunch	10–20	braised, creamed
Corn, canned	1 can		pudding
Cucumber	1 small	10–15	creamed, sautéed
Eggplant	1 very small	10–15	fried, baked

TOO BIG EXCEPT FOR ENTERTAINING

Broccoli	1 bunch serves 4	10–30	baked with cheese
Brussels sprouts	1 lb. serves 4	10–15	baked with cheese
Cabbage	1 average head serves 4	5–15	cole slaw, baked with cheese
Frozen vegetables	1 package serves 3		

*Onions, potatoes, and tomatoes can be bought in larger quantities, as they keep well; buy 1 pound of small white onions, 2 or 3 pounds of potatoes, 1 or 2 pounds of tomatoes.

Green beans, Brussels sprouts, corn, peas, spinach, and sweet potatoes keep the least well.

———·———

LEFTOVER VEGETABLES

For Cream Soups

Cooked lima beans, carrots, cauliflower, celery, corn, mushrooms, onions, potatoes, peas, spinach, tomatoes.

For Clear Soups

Cooked cabbage, beets, onions, or any mixed bits, added to stock.

For Salads

Cooked asparagus, green beans, lima beans, beets, carrots, potatoes, peas.

Raw cabbage, carrots, cauliflower, celery, cucumbers, onions, tomatoes, peppers, radishes, mushrooms, zucchini, lettuce, and other greens.

———————

Artichokes

Cut off the bottom stem almost to the base of the leaves and also cut off about an inch through the leaves at the top. Cook in enough boiling salted water to cover. Boil uncovered for 30 to 45 minutes until the bottom can be pierced easily with a fork. Drain well and serve with hot melted butter or hollandaise. Or serve the heart cold with mayonnaise. Frozen artichoke or canned hearts are good either hot or in salad.

Asparagus

Choose good stalks with firm, upright heads. Snap off the white, tough ends and discard. Soak the stalks for a few minutes in warm water to remove grit. Scrape the stems with a vegetable peeler or sharp knife to remove the little leaves. Place in boiling water with the heads up and not covered and cook for 10 minutes, or less if stems are less than about a dime in diameter. Then submerge the whole stalks and cook for 5 more minutes. Drain immediately to avoid overcooking. Serve with melted butter or hollandaise. Use cold in salad with French dressing.

Asparagus Soufflé

Combine 1 egg yolk with ½ can condensed cream of asparagus soup. Beat 1 egg white until very stiff and fold gently into the soup mixture. Put in a greased baking dish; set the dish in a pan of hot water. Bake in a 350° F. oven for 35 to 40 minutes, until puffy and firm.

Baked Beans

The homemade kind is entirely too much trouble for one person. Buy canned beans without tomato sauce, put in a casserole, and mix in ½ tablespoon of molasses and a pinch of dried mustard. Top with a small onion, quartered, and 2 strips of bacon, and bake until brown and crisp on top. Vary this by adding two or three frankfurters cut in pieces, or Vienna sausage, instead of the bacon. This makes a hearty one-dish meal with salad on the side. A small can makes 2 servings.

Lima Beans

Fresh lima beans are rarely seen in supermarkets nowadays. Frozen ones are among the most successful of frozen vegetables. They come in two sizes, baby and Fordhook. My preference is for the big Fordhooks, which taste more like the ones we used to grow.

Green Beans

Cut off the ends and slice lengthwise with a special cutter or a sharp knife. Cook in boiling water, uncovered, adding salt after the first 10 minutes. Young beans will be cooked in 15 minutes, older ones in 20 to 30 minutes. Serve with butter and plenty of freshly ground black pepper. Use cold in salad with French dressing and a little minced onion. Frozen Italian beans are very tender. Cook very briefly and serve at once.

Beets

Buy *small* beets or else get canned ones, which are excellent. Scrub fresh beets well, but do not pare or scrape. Leave about an inch of stem attached. Cook in boiling salted water, covered, for 20 to 40 minutes, depending on size. Drain, put in cold water for a minute or two, and then slip off the skins. Serve with butter, either whole or sliced. Save the cooking water for borscht. Use leftovers in salad.

Harvard Beets

Make a sauce of 1 teaspoon cornstarch, 1 tablespoon sugar, 2 tablespoons vinegar, and 2 tablespoons beet cooking water; bring slowly to a boil; add ½ cup cooked diced beets; simmer until thoroughly heated; add 1 tablespoon butter just before serving.

Beet Greens

Wash thoroughly and cook uncovered in a small amount of boiling salted water until tender, about 15 minutes. Drain well, chop, and serve with butter and a tablespoon of cream.

Broccoli

Cut off the leaves and the tough part of the stalk. Soak in cold salted water for at least 15 minutes. Cook in plenty of boiling water, uncovered. Add salt after the first 10 minutes. Cook 10 to 25 minutes, depending on size and age. Test the stems with a fork for tenderness. Drain well and serve with melted butter or hollandaise. Leftovers can be baked in a casserole with cream sauce and grated cheese. Add leftover chicken to this for a one-dish meal.

Broccoli with Blue Cheese

Cook 1 package frozen broccoli spears according to package directions. Mix 1½ tablespoons salad oil, 1 tablespoon vinegar, and 1 tablespoon sugar in a small saucepan and heat to boiling point. Remove from heat and crumble 1 ounce blue cheese into the mixture. Pour over the broccoli and sprinkle with paprika.

Brussels Sprouts

Remove any wilted leaves or stems and leave whole. Soak 30 minutes in cold salted water. Cook in plenty of boiling salted water, uncovered, for 15 to 25 minutes. Test with a fork for tenderness. Drain well and serve with melted butter or holland-aise. Leftovers can be dipped in a little salted cream and baked in a shallow greased dish with grated cheese sprinkled on top.

Cabbage

Choose as small a head as possible. Strip off any wilted leaves, cut in quarters, and soak half an hour in cold salted water. Cook in plenty of boiling salted water, uncovered, for 10 to 20 minutes. Do not overcook—it should still be a little crisp when taken off the fire. Drain and serve with butter or cream sauce. Leftovers can be creamed and baked in a casserole with grated cheese. Or, cook only half the head and save the rest for cole slaw (see p. 114).

Skillet Cabbage

Coarsely chop half a small head of cabbage. Melt 2 tablespoons bacon grease in a *heavy* skillet; add the cabbage and ¼ cup water. Mix, cover, and cook 10 minutes over medium-low heat. Add salt and pepper and an 8-ounce carton of sour cream. Simmer until hot. When reheating use a double boiler—the cabbage will brown if done in the skillet again.

Carrots

Choose small carrots or else buy in cans, julienne style. Cut off the tops, scrape with a special scraper or a sharp knife, and leave whole or quarter them, slice, dice, or cut into thin strips. Cook in a small amount of boiling salted water, covered, for 15 to 25 minutes, depending on whether cut or whole. Serve with butter, pepper, and chopped parsley. Leftovers can be served mashed, riced, or glazed; or cook only half the bunch and save the rest to eat raw, either grated or cut in strips. Carrots and peas are a familiar combination; others are carrots and diced celery, cooked together, carrots and finely chopped white onion, carrots and diced cucumber.

Glazed Carrots

Make a syrup by cooking together for 5 minutes 2 tablespoons brown sugar, 1 tablespoon butter, and 1 tablespoon hot water. Pour this over whole cooked carrots in a shallow dish and bake in a 375° F. oven until brown, about 15 minutes.

Cauliflower

Cut off the stalk and all the green leaves. Soak, head down, in cold salted water for 30 minutes. Cook covered in plenty of boiling salted water for 20 to 30 minutes. Test the stalk base with a fork for tenderness, and do not let it overcook or get mushy. Serve with cream sauce, or melted butter in which bread crumbs have been browned, or hollandaise. Leftovers can be used with an alternate sauce or baked with cream sauce and plenty of grated cheese. Or bake in a casserole with shrimps.

Celery

Pull the stalks apart and wash well with a vegetable brush. Save the outside stalks for cooking and the heart to eat raw. Save the leaves for soups and stews. To cook, cut stalks in half-inch pieces, taking off the tough strings as you do so. Boil covered in salted water until soft, 15 to 20 minutes. Serve with butter or cream sauce and paprika.

Braised Celery

Cut the stalks in 4-inch lengths. Melt 1 tablespoon butter in a frying pan; add celery, salt, and pepper. Cover and cook slowly for 10 minutes. Remove the cover, increase the heat, and brown well, turning frequently to brown evenly. When brown, pour over ¼ cup bouillon, reduce heat, and simmer until most of the juice is absorbed, about 10 minutes.

Corn

Remove husks and silk, and cut the stem close to the end of the ear. Cook covered in boiling water, 6 to 15 minutes, depending on age. Do not add salt. Remove from the heat when a fork can just pierce a kernel easily. Serve, either on or off the cob, with butter, salt, and paprika. Use leftovers with lima beans as succotash, or in cream of corn soup.

Canned corn comes in two styles, creamed or in kernels. The kernel kind is simply heated and served with butter, salt, and pepper. Try the white shoe-peg variety for a change—the tiny kernels have a sweet, delicate flavor.

Corn Pudding

Make a cream sauce of 1 tablespoon butter, 1 tablespoon flour, and ¾ cup milk: melt the butter, stir in the flour, then stir in the milk until sauce is thickened. Season, and add 1 egg, well beaten, and 1 cup cream-style corn, drained. Blend thoroughly and put in a greased casserole. Bake in a 350° F. oven for 30 to 40 minutes, until the pudding is set.

Cucumbers

Pare cucumbers, slice in half lengthwise, remove seeds, and cut in ¼-inch slices. Boil uncovered in a small amount of water 10 to 15 minutes until tender. Drain well and serve with sour cream or cream sauce. Or sauté until tender in melted butter with plenty of seasonings. Raw cucumbers pared and sliced very thin and combined with French dressing go particularly well with fish.

Fried Cucumber Strips

Peel a cucumber, cut in half lengthwise, and remove seeds. Cut into strips about ½ inch wide. Sprinkle with salt and pepper. Roll in flour, dip in 1 well-beaten egg, and roll in bread or cracker crumbs. Refrigerate 30 minutes or longer, to set the coating.

Heat vegetable oil, about ¼ inch deep in the pan, and quickly fry the strips, turning to brown. Don't crowd in the skillet. Dry on paper towels.

Fried Eggplant

For fried slices, peel and cut ½ inch thick. Dredge lightly with flour and fry in melted bacon fat over moderate heat until golden brown. Turn once, and season each side with salt and pepper.

Baked Eggplant

Use half of a medium-size eggplant. Peel and cut in 1-inch cubes, and cook 15 minutes, covered, in boiling salted water. Drain well. While this is cooking, sauté in butter 1 small onion, minced, and 1 tablespoon minced green pepper. Combine with the eggplant and 1 tomato, sliced, and salt and pepper. Put in a greased casserole, top with bread crumbs and grated cheese, and dot with butter. Bake in a 400° F. oven for 30 minutes, until the cheese is melted and the top is brown. This makes 2 servings.

Braised Endive

Sauté 2 stalks endive in 2 tablespoons butter over low heat until soft. Sprinkle with freshly ground black pepper. Add ⅓ cup well-seasoned chicken bouillon. Cover and heat slowly. Cook about 20 minutes, turning once.

Mushrooms

Choose medium to large mushrooms, so as to get more cap in proportion to the stem by weight. Snap off the stems and save them for soup, egg dishes, or casseroles. If the skins are dark, peel off with your fingers; otherwise wipe off the tops with a damp cloth and leave the skin on. Sauté in butter for 10 to 15 minutes, turning to cook both sides. Serve with bacon on toast as a main dish.

To cream, sauté first, remove the mushrooms, and in the same pan blend 1 tablespoon flour with 2 tablespoons butter, using what is left from cooking the mushrooms. Add ¼ cup milk slowly and stir until the sauce thickens. Season with salt, pepper, and ½ teaspoon sherry, put back the mushrooms, and heat thoroughly. Serve on toast or in a patty shell.

Slice and chop stems in blender; add to omelets or scrambled eggs or canned spaghetti with meat sauce.

Onions

For one-person cookery, always buy small white onions, 1 pound at a time. They will keep well in a cool, dark place and are constantly needed in cooking. Always cut and peel under cold water. If your fingers retain the smell even with this precaution, rub them lightly on a kitchen deodorizer such as Airwick. For seasoning in cooking, cut very fine or chop. If a recipe calls for onion juice, get the bottled kind.

To boil onions, peel and leave whole. Cook for 20 to 30 minutes, covered, until just tender. Serve with butter or cream sauce or condensed cream of celery soup.

To fry, cut in ⅛-inch slices and fry over moderate heat in butter or bacon fat about 15 minutes. Be careful not to let them burn. French fried onions are available frozen and in cans.

Most salads are improved by a touch of onion. A minced white onion will do, but chopped chives or scallions are more delicate.

Peas

Shell just before cooking. Cook in a very small amount of water, 1 cup to 1 pound of peas. Cook in boiling salted water, uncovered, for 10 to 20 minutes. Serve with butter, salt, and pepper. Leftovers can be used with soup, mixed vegetable salad, or any creamed dish, especially creamed fish or chicken. Snow peas (frozen) are very delicate.

Peas Bonne Femme

Shell 1 pound peas, peel 6 small white onions, put them in a saucepan, and cover with 2 or 3 large lettuce leaves. Add 2 tablespoons butter and ¼ cup water. Cover and cook slowly for about 30 minutes, until the peas are tender. Add ½ cup light cream and salt, and serve as soon as the cream is very hot. This is simply delicious and no trouble at all. This amount serves 2.

Green Peppers

Generally used as stuffed peppers, but they are good for flavoring in soups, stews, and casseroles, and grated raw in salads. In any case, cut out the stem and remove the seeds and white membranes. Before stuffing, cover with boiling water and let stand 15 minutes to soften. Drain well, fill with the stuffing, and place upright in a deep baking dish. Put an inch of tomato sauce or hot water in the bottom of the dish and bake uncovered in a 375° F. oven for about 30 minutes.

For stuffing use corned or roast beef hash; leftover rice or spaghetti combined with ground meat (either raw or cooked), minced onion, and seasonings; or ¼ pound ground meat mixed well with bread crumbs and chopped onion, well seasoned with salt, pepper, Worcestershire sauce, and a pinch of dried herbs.

Potatoes

Buy 2 or 3 pounds if you use potatoes frequently, otherwise less. Idaho potatoes are best for baking, and little new potatoes for boiling—cook unpeeled and eat them skins and all. Ordinary Irish potatoes can be cooked in any way. Canned potatoes save time for stews and casseroles. Potato chips can be heated in the oven and used as a garnish for a quick meal. Shoestring potatoes, which come in cans, are heated in the same way and are even better than chips, also a little more substantial.

To boil potatoes, scrub well and do not peel. Cook in enough boiling salted water to cover, with the lid on, for 20 to 30 minutes, until tender when tested with a fork. Drain immediately, put the potatoes back in the pot, cover, leaving a crack for steam to escape, and put over very low heat for 5 to 10 minutes before serving. Peel and serve with butter and chopped parsley. Leftovers can be mashed, fried, creamed, hashed brown, or used in soup or salad or combined with meat for hash, stuffed peppers, casseroles, or shepherd's pie.

Mashed Potatoes

Boil, drain, and peel. While still hot, put through a ricer, or mash with a masher or fork; be sure to have no lumps. Put in a double boiler over hot water; add butter and hot milk gradually, mixing thoroughly until the potatoes have the right consistency. Season and heat well before serving. Use at least 3 potatoes with 1 tablespoon butter and ¼ cup milk. Mashed potatoes make a good crust for any casserole of meat, fish, or vegetables.

Leftovers can be made into flat cakes and fried in bacon fat, or can be put in a greased dish and browned in the oven. Mashed potatoes are available in dehydrated form, or frozen, ready to heat. A package of dehydrated makes 4 generous servings. Add 1 tablespoon instant onion when mixing.

Fried Potatoes

Slice and brown cold boiled potatoes with a minced onion in hot bacon fat or melted butter. Be careful not to let them stick to the bottom of the pan. French fries can be bought frozen, ready to brown.

Hashed Brown Potatoes

Take 1 or 2 cold boiled potatoes and chop very fine in a chopping bowl. Melt bacon fat, 1 tablespoon for each potato, in a frying pan and put in the potatoes, patting them down to form an even, compact mass. Season and pour over ⅛ cup light cream. Cover and cook over slow heat without stirring until a crust has formed on the bottom—test with a spatula or fork. This will take about 20 minutes. Fold in half like an omelet and take out with a pancake lifter.

Creamed Potatoes

Dice 2 cold boiled potatoes. Melt 1 tablespoon butter in a pan, add the potatoes, and let them get hot and coated with butter but not brown. Season with salt and pepper. Add ½ tablespoon flour and blend thoroughly. Add ½ cup milk slowly, stirring constantly. When this starts to boil, lower the heat and simmer for 5 minutes. Sprinkle with paprika and chopped parsley or chives. Leftovers can be baked in a casserole with grated cheese on top.

Scalloped Potatoes

Peel 2 raw potatoes and cut in ⅛-inch slices. Put a layer of potatoes in a greased casserole. Season and dot generously with butter, and sprinkle a little flour over all. Repeat until the dish is almost full. Pour in ½ cup milk. Do not have the dish too full or the milk will boil over. Bake covered in a 325° F. oven for 30 minutes, then uncover and cook another 20 minutes. The top should have a light brown crust and the potatoes should be tender when tested with a fork. About ½ cup ground cooked ham put between the layers will make a main-course dish.

Baked Potatoes

Use Idahos or large Irish potatoes. New potatoes are not good for baking. Scrub thoroughly and rub the skin with salad oil. Preheat the oven to 400° F. and bake 45 minutes for medium-size, 1 hour for large potatoes. Test for softness by squeezing with your hand wrapped in a cloth, or pierce with fork. Serve with plenty of butter, salt, and paprika.

Stuffed Baked Potatoes

When baked as above, allow to cool somewhat. Then cut a piece of skin out of the flat side, slightly larger than the size of a tablespoon. Scoop out all the inside with a small spoon, being careful not to break the skin. Mash in a bowl with butter, a little warm milk or cream, salt, paprika, a dash of dried sage, and a little minced onion. Put the mixture back in the potato shell and brown in a hot oven for about 10 minutes. A second potato done at the same time can be reheated the following day.

Sweet Potatoes

Choose fat sweet potatoes for the best flavor. If they are very large, half can be saved after cooking and used up in another way. Scrub well, but do not peel. Boil in enough salted water to cover, and cook with the lid on for 20 to 30 minutes, or longer for a larger potato. When done, the skin should be loose and the potato soft. Drain, peel, and serve mashed up with butter and seasonings.

Leftovers can be used by dipping the pieces in flour and frying in bacon fat or butter, browning on both sides; or by mashing thoroughly with butter and then baking in a greased casserole until browned on top. Both canned and frozen sweet potatoes (or yams) can be bought.

Candied Sweet Potatoes

Peel a boiled sweet potato when cool and cut in ½-inch slices. Butter a small casserole, put in a layer of potato, sprinkle with brown sugar and salt, and dot with butter. Repeat until the dish is full. Bake uncovered in a 375° F. oven until potatoes are glazed on top, basting frequently—about 30 minutes.

Spinach

Remove all wilted leaves and snap off the stems at the base of the leaf. Fill a dishpan with warm water, put the spinach in it, and immerse for a few minutes. Take out the spinach and then empty the pan, which will probably contain sand and dirt. Repeat four or five times with fresh water until the water stays clean. Cook the spinach uncovered in a small amount of boiling salted water, about ½ cup to 1 pound, for about 10 minutes. Drain thoroughly, squeezing out the water through a sieve. Chop fine in a chopping bowl and reheat with butter or medium white sauce (p. 141), about ¼ cup sauce to 1 cup of cooked spinach, or combine with ½ can undiluted cream of mushroom soup. Add a dash of nutmeg as well as salt and pepper. Leftovers can be used for cream of spinach soup or with egg dishes.

Spinach Soufflé

Combine 1 jar strained baby-food spinach with 1 cup thick white sauce (p. 141). Add necessary seasonings and a dash of nutmeg. Beat in 1 egg yolk. Beat 1 egg white until very stiff and fold gently into the spinach mixture. Put in a greased baking dish; set the dish in a pan of water. Bake in a 350° F. oven 35 to 40 minutes, until puffy and firm. Easier yet, buy the excellent frozen soufflé that serves 2 and can be reheated.

Acorn Squash

Cut in half lengthwise and scrape out the seeds and pith. Put in a baking pan with about ½ inch of water in the pan. Put a generous lump of butter in the squash, about 1 teaspoon, and sprinkle with salt and pepper. Or put in 2 link sausages or a cake of sausage meat. Bake 50 to 60 minutes in a 375° F. oven. Cook both halves, as one will reheat satisfactorily if not refrigerated. Hubbard squash has a similar flavor but is entirely too large to be practicable. It can be bought frozen, ready to heat with plenty of butter, salt, and pepper. Serve like mashed sweet potatoes.

Summer Squash

Choose the long yellow kind, about ½ pound for 1 serving, rather than the round white patty-pan variety, which is usually too big. Wash, do not peel, and slice or cube. Cook in boiling salted water, covered, for 10 to 15 minutes, until tender. Serve with butter and freshly ground black pepper, or with a thin white sauce. Or sauté until tender in melted butter.

Zucchini

Wash, do not peel, and cut in ¼-inch slices. Cook the same way as yellow summer squash or combine the two. Can also be cooked with chopped scallions and diced peeled tomatoes.

Zucchini with Herbs

Melt 1 teaspoon butter and 1 teaspoon olive oil together. Add 1 very small clove of garlic, minced, and ½ teaspoon onion flakes. Cook over low heat for 10 minutes. Cut 1 small or ½ medium-size zucchini (not peeled) into ¼-inch slices. Add to the other ingredients in the pan and season with salt, pepper, and a pinch each of chopped parsley and marjoram, and 1 tablespoon hot water. Cover and cook until tender, about 15 minutes. Stir in some grated Parmesan cheese, and serve.

Baked Zucchini

Slice one zucchini in half lengthwise and then crosswise. Parboil the four pieces. Drain and place in a shallow baking dish with ½ teaspoon butter on each piece. Season with salt and pepper. Sprinkle liberally with paprika and grated Parmesan cheese. Bake in a 350° F. oven for 10 minutes. Zucchini are so easy to prepare and quick-cooking that only fresh ones are recommended; the frozen variety saves no time or trouble and is mushy.

Stuffed Zucchini

Choose fairly large zucchini, slice in half lengthwise and parboil. Scoop out the seeds. Fill the hollows with cooked ground beef or lamb, seasoned with salt and pepper. Cover the meat with mashed potato and dust the top with grated cheese (any kind). Bake in 350° F. oven until thoroughly heated and cheese is well melted.

Stewed Tomatoes

Remove the stem, and skin the tomatoes by letting them stand a few minutes in boiling water. The skin will then come off very easily. Sauté 1 small minced onion in 1 tablespoon butter. Add 2 or 3 tomatoes, peeled and sliced; season and simmer them for 15 minutes. Make a smooth paste of 1 tablespoon flour in a little water and add to the tomatoes, stirring until thickened. Leftovers can be used for cream of tomato soup or for **scalloped tomatoes**: combine with soft bread crumbs and bake in a casserole 20 minutes in a moderate oven, until browned on top.

Broiled Tomato

Cut a medium-size ripe tomato in half. Place on a pan, cut side up. Sprinkle over the top of each half a mixture of 1 tablespoon seasoned bread crumbs, 1 tablespoon instant onion flakes, 1 tablespoon softened butter, and ½ teaspoon basil. Put under the broiler for about 10 minutes, until the crumbs are well browned. Watch carefully so as not to burn.

Tomato and Rice Casserole

Slice 1 medium-size tomato, fry in bacon grease, dust with flour, and season with salt, pepper, and a pinch of basil. Put about 1 cup of cooked rice in a greased baking dish and put the tomato slices on top. Cover with ½ can condensed Cheddar cheese soup and heat in 325° F. oven until bubbling. Top with slices of crisp cooked bacon and keep warm in the oven until ready to serve.

Fried Tomatoes and Bacon

Fry 2 slices of bacon, remove from heat, put on a hot plate, and cover. Pour off all the grease except just enough to coat the bottom of the pan. Put in it 2 small tomatoes, sliced but not peeled. Season and fry until soft on both sides but still firm enough to remove unbroken with a pancake lifter. The end pieces with the skin on will take a little longer than the middle pieces. Put on the same covered plate with the bacon. Add 1 teaspoon flour to the liquid remaining in the pan, and add a scant ¼ cup water, just enough to cover the bottom of the pan. Stir over medium heat until the gravy thickens, 2 or 3 minutes. Pour over the tomatoes and serve.

Vegetable Casserole

Line a greased baking dish with a layer of cold boiled rice, add a layer of thinly sliced zucchini and chopped onions, and then a layer of sliced or canned tomatoes. Season with salt, pepper, and a little basil. Repeat until the dish is full, ending with tomatoes on top. Pour in 1 cup of bouillon. Sprinkle the top with grated cheese and bake in a 350° F. oven until vegetables are tender.

Variation: This recipe can be varied by adding finely chopped green pepper and a small can of whole-kernel corn. Any leftover cooked green vegetable such as peas, lima beans, or green beans can be added, or diced cold meat or chicken. Macaroni can be substituted for rice.

Creamed or Scalloped Vegetables

Leftover vegetables can be creamed or scalloped—that is, mixed with cream sauce, either alone or in combination with two or more vegetables. Put in a greased baking dish and top with bread crumbs and dot with butter or sprinkle with grated cheese. Bake in a 375° F. oven until well heated. Creamed mixed vegetables can also be served as shortcake, between halves of large baking powder biscuits.

12

SALADS

THE BEST POSSIBLE SALAD—and to many people the only kind
—is a bowl of mixed greens with French dressing. A single person, however, is probably not going to buy lettuce, chicory, watercress, and so on just for two or three servings, so unless you
have access to a garden you will have to curb your enthusiasm
for a profusion of greens. Lettuce does keep surprisingly well,
and does come in small heads, particularly Boston or romaine.
Chicory or romaine, which looks like a lot, does not always yield
much from one head. Endive is usually sold by weight, and ¼
pound goes a long way. You can treat yourself to an occasional
bunch of watercress even if some of it is wasted.

Otherwise, unless you are a purist about greens, salads are an
economical way of using up small leftovers of fish, vegetables,
and fruit, and they can also serve in a number of ways as an
alternative to dessert. Toss in some little extras to add variety—
croutons, bacon bits, chopped hard-boiled egg, olive slices, strips
of cheese or ham.

SALADS WITH VEGETABLES

Mixed Green Salad

Rub a wooden bowl with a cut clove of garlic. Shred into small pieces with your fingers several lettuce leaves and whatever other greens you may wish. Fresh herbs, if available, may be added very judiciously. Pour in 1 or 2 tablespoons of French dressing, according to taste, and toss lightly with a wooden fork and spoon until all the leaves are coated with dressing. A little Roquefort cheese may be crumbled in the dressing, if desired.

Single Vegetables

Asparagus, green beans, tomatoes, avocado, all with French dressing, and potatoes with mayonnaise.

Mixed Raw Vegetables

In addition to lettuce, any of the following vegetables, either alone or in combination, can be used: grated carrots, cauliflower flowerets, chopped celery, sliced cucumber, chopped chives or scallions, tomatoes sliced or quartered, grated green pepper, sliced radishes, mushrooms, zucchini. Use a French dressing.

Russian Salad

Combine any cooked vegetables such as peas, green beans, potato, carrots, lima beans, or use a small can of mixed vegetables. Add finely chopped scallions and the essential ingredient, diced beets. Mix with Russian dressing (p. 121) and serve on lettuce.

Cole Slaw

Shred as much raw cabbage as you want and mix with mayonnaise. Add a little grated carrot. This is the easiest of many ways to make cole slaw, although most recipes call for boiled dressing.

Another good and easy method is to fry a piece of bacon, diced, add to 2 tablespoons vinegar, heat almost to boiling point, pour over the shredded cabbage, and mix thoroughly.

Stuffed Tomato

Peel a tomato by immersing it for a few minutes in boiling water, then into cold water, and removing the skin. Take out the stem, seeds, and pulp carefully. Fill with one of the following mixtures, chill thoroughly, and serve on one or two lettuce leaves: celery and mayonnaise; chicken, celery, and mayonnaise; apples, celery, and mayonnaise; seafood or fish, celery, and mayonnaise; chopped egg, celery, and mayonnaise.

Stuffed Avocado

Cut the avocado in half and remove the pit. Heap the center with seafood and Russian dressing, or grapefruit sections and French dressing. There is nothing better than an avocado by itself, either removed from its shell and sliced on lettuce or simply served with French dressing poured into the hollow left by the pit.

Kidney Bean Salad

Combine well-drained canned kidney beans with peeled and diced cucumber, chopped celery, chopped green pepper, and scallions. Mix with mayonnaise and chill before serving.

Four-Bean Salad

The usual three-bean salad combines cut green beans, baby limas, and red kidney beans. Wax beans could be added, and chickpeas could be substituted for the limas. Mix with French dressing and a dash of tarragon or basil. Decorate, if desired, with rings of thinly sliced onion and green pepper.

Beet Salad

Mix cooked or canned beets, diced or in julienne strips, with finely chopped scallions and parsley. Add French dressing. Cover and refrigerate several hours before serving or overnight. Before serving stir gently and check for seasoning.

Also good with beets is a dressing made with yogurt: combine 1 tablespoon each olive oil and lemon juice and salt to taste with ½ cup plain yogurt.

Chickpea Salad

Combine cooked or canned chickpeas with about half the amount of chopped celery, a little chopped pimiento, and green pepper. Mix with mayonnaise to which has been added a dash of prepared horseradish. Serve on lettuce.

Cucumber and Yogurt

Peel and quarter a small cucumber, removing seeds if large. Combine 1 cup plain yogurt with 2 finely chopped scallions, including part of the green tops, a little salt, and ½ teaspoon ground cumin. Stir in the cucumber and chill well.

Cucumber in Sour Cream

Combine ¼ cup sour cream with 3 tablespoons white wine vinegar, ½ teaspoon salt, and a little white pepper. Peel and thinly slice a cucumber, finely chop 4 or 5 scallions, and toss with the dressing. Cover and chill at least 1 hour. Toss again, drain, and serve. Chopped chives could be sprinkled on top.

Potato Salad

There must be enough recipes for potato salad to fill a book. The one I like adds to the diced potatoes some chopped celery, chopped hard-boiled egg, and a spoonful of sweet pickle relish. Combine with mayonnaise and dust liberally with paprika.

Spinach Salad and Mushrooms

Remove stems from spinach, wash well, and drain. Break into bite-size pieces and put in a bowl. Add mushrooms, sliced thin. Cook 2 or 3 strips of bacon until crisp and drain on a paper towel. Add 3 tablespoons red vinegar to the bacon fat and allow to cool. Break up the bacon over the spinach and mushrooms, season with pepper—but no salt—and toss with the dressing.

Zucchini Salad

Raw zucchini sliced paper-thin is a good addition to any green salad combination. Try it with radishes, celery, green pepper, onion, and diced apple, in a French dressing.

MISCELLANEOUS SALADS

Jellied Pâté

Take an individual ring mold and fill ⅓ full of canned jellied consommé while still liquid. Allow this to jell slightly in the refrigerator—about 45 minutes—and when it starts to set spread generously but gently with liver pâté. Cover this with more consommé to fill the mold and allow to jell thoroughly for 3 or 4 hours. Unmold on to shredded lettuce and fill the middle with a mixture of chopped hard-boiled egg, celery, and mayonnaise.

This is a good hot-weather dish and should be made the night before unless you have time in the morning.

Sardine and Egg

Mix chopped hard-boiled egg with small pieces of sardines (or anchovies) and mayonnaise and serve on lettuce leaves.

Seafood Salad

Mix any leftover seafood or fish, such as salmon or tuna, with chopped celery and mayonnaise and serve on lettuce leaves.

Basic Aspic

Dissolve ½ envelope unflavored gelatin in ¼ cup cold water. Add ⅝ cup hot bouillon or tomato juice. Cool and allow to thicken a little. Then stir in 1 cup of any of these: diced chicken; flaked tuna, crabmeat, or lobster; chopped raw vegetables, cabbage, celery, carrots, green pepper, cucumber. Chopped hard-boiled egg or olives may also be added with the chicken, seafood, or vegetables. This amount fills 2 custard cups.

For jellied fruit salads, add hot fruit juice instead of the bouillon or use fruit-flavored gelatin; then add fresh or canned fruit in whatever combination you wish. A good one is lime gelatin with pears, white grapes, and grapefruit segments. (Frozen fruit is too soft to use in jelly.)

Tomato Aspic

Put 2 tablespoons tomato juice in an individual mold and fill the mold with jellied madrilène while still liquid. Season well, mix, and chill in the refrigerator for about 3 hours or until jellied. Serve on lettuce with mayonnaise or a mixture of chopped celery, apples, and mayonnaise.

A very good tomato aspic can be bought in cans, about three

portions to the can. Serve on lettuce with mayonnaise with chicken, egg, tuna, or seafood salad; apple and celery salad; or with "garden salad" cottage cheese.

Egg in Aspic

Make a basic aspic with chicken bouillon as above, using half the quantity. Pour about ¾ inch into a custard cup and set this in the refrigerator to jell (about 1 hour). Meanwhile, poach 1 egg so that the white is firm and the yolk soft. Allow it to cool. When jelly is somewhat firm, spread it with 1 tablespoon liver pâté, put the egg on top of the pâté, sprinkle with salt and pepper, and add a little tarragon. Pour over the rest of the liquid and cool until firm. Serve with sprigs of crisp watercress.

Chicken Waldorf Salad

Peel and slice 1 small apple; sprinkle with lemon juice. Combine with diced chicken, finely chopped celery, seedless white grapes, and some chopped walnuts. Mix well with mayonnaise or sour cream.

Chef's Salad

Combine julienne strips of boiled ham, chicken, tongue, and Swiss-type cheese. Use your favorite dressing and serve on lettuce. Or use just the ham and cheese with onion rings and strips of green pepper, but this should have only a simple oil and vinegar dressing.

Shrimp Louis

Arrange shelled and cleaned boiled shrimp on a bed of shredded lettuce. Garnish with hearts of artichoke, sliced hard-boiled eggs, and peeled tomato quarters. Pour on a Louis dressing—equal parts of mayonnaise, French dressing, and chili sauce.

Salade Niçoise

There are many recipes for this traditional French salad. All agree on anchovies, tomatoes, scallions, black olives, basil, and an olive oil dressing made with garlic and little if no vinegar. Green beans and boiled new potatoes may be added, also tuna, even a little minced green pepper and celery. Try your own combination. It's better with garden-fresh tomatoes, but cherry tomatoes can substitute.

Danish Macaroni Salad

Cook elbow macaroni according to package directions and allow to cool. Combine with finely chopped boiled ham and 1 tablespoon diced pimiento. For the dressing, mash the yolk of a hard-boiled egg in a bowl; add a little dry mustard and salt to taste. Gradually mix in 1 tablespoon mayonnaise and then 2 tablespoons sour cream. Mix with the macaroni, cover, and chill.

Rice Salad

To a cup of cooked rice add some shredded carrot, finely chopped small onion or 2 scallions, green pepper, celery, and parsley, all chopped fine. Toss with French dressing and chill. Tuna could be added to make a one-dish meal.

Rice and Beet Salad

Combine ½ cup cooked rice with ½ cup diced beets and 2 finely chopped scallions. Mix with 2 tablespoons French dressing. Cover and chill several hours or overnight. When ready to serve add a few cooked green beans or peas, carrots, and diced chicken. Sprinkle with chives and parsley and mix with mayonnaise or more French dressing.

Summer Salad

Arrange the following, in the order given, around a large dinner plate: shredded lettuce, grated carrots, sliced cucumbers, sliced tomatoes, cold cooked asparagus or green beans, deviled eggs, 1 or 2 rolled slices of cold boiled ham. Put a mound of cottage cheese mixed with chives in the center. Refrigerate for about an hour. Just before serving, moisten each of the vegetables except the carrots with French dressing.

Fruit Salads

The following combinations are very good:

- Grapefruit and avocado with French dressing.
- Pears and cream cheese and French dressing. (Try adding some chopped crystallized ginger.)
- Pineapple and cottage cheese and French dressing.
- Mixed fruit and cream mayonnaise.
- Canned freestone peaches and cottage cheese.
- Bing cherries with cream cheese and French dressing.

A fruit salad which I enjoyed in California with the temperature at 110° F. is made this way:

Put a good helping of cottage cheese on a bed of shredded lettuce and surround with drained canned fruit—half a pear, half a peach, half an apricot, a fig, a prune, a slice of pineapple (or make your own selection). Serve without dressing and *very* cold. Buy the smallest size cans of fruit and use up leftovers in fruit compote or jelly.

Orange and Onion Salad

Peel a California orange, removing all white membranes, and cut in thick slices. Peel a large Bermuda onion and slice very thin. Marinate in French dressing for an hour or so. Drain and serve on lettuce. This goes well with egg and cheese dishes.

SALAD DRESSINGS

Salad dressings can make or mar the salad, but you cannot go wrong with a simple French dressing mixed according to instructions. You *must* use real olive oil—it is expensive but nothing else can substitute successfully. Good mayonnaise comes prepared in jars and is much less trouble—and expense—than making it yourself. Be sure to buy a product labeled *mayonnaise* and not just *salad dressing.* If you have a blender, make your own.

French Dressing

¼ cup olive oil
2 tablespoons vinegar
⅓ teaspoon salt
⅛ teaspoon pepper
pinch of dry mustard

Mix thoroughly with a fork in a small bowl or put in a covered jar and shake well just before using. For a more pungent dressing, add a pinch of herbs (p. 21) or 1 tablespoon crumbled Roquefort or blue cheese. Commercial blue cheese dressing has a creamier consistency.

Low-Calorie French Dressing

Combine 1 cup plain yogurt, chilled, with 2 tablespoons olive oil, 2 tablespoons lemon juice, salt, and pepper, and mix thoroughly.

Russian Dressing

Add 3 tablespoons chili sauce to ⅓ cup of beaten mayonnaise. Mix thoroughly.

Cottage Cheese Dressing

½ cup cottage cheese
½ cup milk
1 teaspoon salt
1 teaspoon paprika
2 tablespoons lemon juice
¼ teaspoon minced garlic
½ green pepper, cut in strips
4 radishes, sliced
2 green onions, including tops, coarsely cut

Cover and blend on high speed until vegetables are finely chopped.

Sour Cream and Roquefort Dressing

Mash 2 ounces Roquefort cheese in a small bowl and gradually add 1 cup sour cream. When smooth add 1 teaspoon finely chopped onions or scallions, ½ teaspoon salt, and ½ teaspoon dry mustard and mix thoroughly. Serve on mixed greens or sliced tomatoes. Makes about 1½ cups.

Cream Mayonnaise

Add 3 tablespoons whipped cream to ⅓ cup mayonnaise. Use with fruit salads.

13

⊛

DESSERTS

ELABORATE DESSERTS, the crowning touch of a party dinner, are not part of the picture when cooking for one. They take time and trouble much better spent on the main dish and are likely to require expensive ingredients, especially heavy cream. If you must have pastry or ice cream, the best plan is to bring something home from a bakery or frozen food counter; an occasional tart or éclair can be a pleasant change on any menu.

Fruit is recommended as the best way to end any meal, not only because it tastes good but because it is probably best for your digestion and figure as well. Fresh fruit is preferable, and it is generally possible to find a choice in market even in the middle of winter. It is also easy to buy in very small quantities and should be bought sparingly, as it will not keep long and its flavor is not improved by refrigeration. Keep fruit in a cool place outside the refrigerator and refrigerate only if it is beginning to get overripe. Bananas will turn black in the refrigerator but are still edible.

Fresh fruit is delicious when eaten plain, or peeled and cut and dusted with powdered sugar, or mixed with other fruit; berries, bananas, and peaches are good with sugar and cream. Honey is good as a flavoring, but remember it has twice the sweetening power of sugar. Shredded coconut mixes well with citrus fruit. Raw fruit can be dressed up with a tablespoon of wine, and cooked fruit can be served with custard sauce or cream. Leftover bits of fruit can be combined for fruit jellies or salads.

Whipped cream is available in a mix or in a pressure can; both keep longer than the fresh. Sour cream keeps longer than fresh.

BUYING GUIDE FOR FRESH FRUIT

Fruit	Quantity	How to Use
Apples	1 lb. (3–4)	raw or cooked
Apricots	2–6	raw
Bananas	2–6	raw or cooked
Berries	1 pt.	raw or cooked
Cherries	½–1 lb.	raw
Grapefruit	1–2	raw or broiled
Grapes	½–1 lb.	raw
Melons (cantaloupe, honeyball, or tiny watermelon)	1	raw
Oranges	1 doz.	raw
Peaches	2–6	raw or cooked
Pears	2–6	raw or cooked
Pineapple	usually too large	raw
Plums	2–6	raw or stewed

FRESH FRUIT

Applesauce

Cut 2 medium-sized apples into small pieces, skins, core, and all; add ½ cup water and cook covered over moderate heat 10 minutes or until apples are soft and mushy. Watch out that the bottom does not scorch. Remove from the fire, put through a coarse sieve, and add 2 tablespoons sugar or honey while still hot. A dash of cinnamon and nutmeg may be added also. Leftover sauce can be mixed with the stiffly beaten white of an egg—1 cup of sauce to 1 egg white—and 1 teaspoon lemon juice to make **apple snow**. Use also for applesauce cake and with duck or pork.

Baked Apples

Buy large cooking apples, as they tend to shrink in baking. Core with an apple corer and cut off about an inch of skin on each end. Fill the hole with 1 teaspoon butter and as much sugar, either brown or white, as you can pack in. Set the apple in a pan with ¼ inch water in the bottom. Cover and bake in a 375° F. oven for 30 to 35 minutes until apples are soft. Serve hot or cold, with or without cream. The filling in the center can be varied with the addition of ¼ teaspoon cinnamon, ⅛ teaspoon cloves, and ⅛ teaspoon nutmeg, and with a few nuts and raisins, chopped.

Apple Betty

Trim the crusts from 3 slices of whole wheat bread and cut the bread into small squares. Sauté until brown on both sides in 2 tablespoons melted butter. Peel 2 small apples, core, and cut into small pieces. Mix ⅓ cup sugar with ½ teaspoon cinnamon and ½ teaspoon nutmeg. Squeeze the juice of 1 small lemon. Fill a small greased baking dish with layers of apple, then bread, then the sugar mixture. Sprinkle each time with a little lemon juice. Top with crumbs made from the crust and mixed with the remaining spiced sugar. Grate some lemon rind on top, and pour over the rest of the lemon juice and ¼ cup water. Bake 30 minutes in a 300° F. oven, covered, and then 10 minutes more uncovered to brown the top. This makes two generous servings but is so good that it can be eaten with relish the second time. Serve with cream or hard sauce.

Scalloped Apples

Peel, core, and slice 2 large cooking apples and put in a buttered baking dish. Dot liberally with butter, sprinkle with brown sugar and cinnamon, and add ¼ cup water. Bake about 35 minutes at 350° F. This is a good accompaniment for pork chops, ham, or sausage.

Baked Bananas

Peel a banana, then cut it in half lengthwise and crosswise, making four pieces. Put in a well-greased shallow baking dish, sprinkle with lemon juice and brown sugar, and dot with butter. Then sprinkle with 1 tablespoon rum or sherry and bake in a 375° F. oven for 20 minutes until thoroughly cooked. Be careful not to use overripe bananas for baking.

Banana Custard

Make vanilla pudding from a mix as directed (2 servings). While still warm and soft, add a 7½-ounce jar baby-food strained bananas and blend well. Shredded coconut can also be added. Chill until firm and serve with cream.

Sliced Bananas

Serve with a sprinkling of brown sugar and plenty of cream. Or combine with orange and grapefruit segments with plenty of juice to which some sherry might be added. Or combine with seedless green grapes and sprinkle with orange juice.

Fresh Berries

Crush, sweeten, and serve on biscuits as shortcake. If the berries are starting to get overripe, pick out the best ones and stew with a little sugar, or make into fruit sauce.

Blueberry Pudding

Cook 1½ cups fresh blueberries with ¼ cup water and ⅝ cup sugar for 10 minutes. Butter 3 slices white bread, crusts removed. Put alternate layers of bread and berries in a square dish. Chill for at least 2 hours and serve with cream. 2 servings.

Blueberry Tart

Fill a tart shell (or a sponge-cake shell) with fresh blueberries and cover with hot raspberry jam. Top with sour cream.

Blueberry or Blackberry Flummery

2 cups berries
¼ cup cornstarch
¾ cup sugar
⅛ teaspoon salt
  juice of ½ lemon

Simmer berries in 1 cup water for 5 minutes. Put through a sieve or use the blender to purée a little at a time. Add enough water to the pulp to make 2½ cups. Mix the cornstarch, sugar, and salt, and add to the berries. Cook, stirring constantly, until the mixture is thick and clear, then add the lemon juice. Cool, stirring occasionally, and then refrigerate. Serve with sweet or sour cream.

Blueberry Jelly

Simmer contents of 1 pint box of blueberries in 1 cup of water for 5 minutes. Purée in blender, a little at a time. This makes about 2 cups of liquid. Add ½ cup water, 3 heaping tablespoons sugar and a dash of salt. Dissolve 1 package unflavored gelatin in the juice of ½ lemon and add to the fruit while still warm. Pour into a bowl and chill. Serve with sweet or sour cream.

Cantaloupe and Berries

Cut a small cantaloupe in half and remove seeds. Fill with strawberries or blueberries and pour over 3 ounces of any fortified wine—sherry, port or Madeira—a few minutes before serving.

Frozen Raspberry Cream

1 small can evaporated milk (⅔ cup)
1 thin slice of lemon
1 package frozen raspberries, thawed

Place all ingredients in the electric blender. Cover and blend on high speed until smooth, about 30 seconds. Pour into an ice-cube tray and freeze.

Chilled Grapefruit

Cut in half and separate the segments with a special knife. Chill. Serve plain, or with sugar or honey, or with a teaspoon of sherry or maraschino.

Broiled Grapefruit

Cut in half, separate the sections, and remove the core. Sprinkle with honey or brown sugar and dot with a little butter. Put in a pan and heat under the broiler, not too close, until browned, about 15 minutes. Add 1 teaspoon of sherry before serving.

Fresh Grapes

Cut in half as many seedless white grapes as you want—about 1 cup per serving—mix with 1 tablespoon chopped fresh mint, and chill 1 to 2 hours before serving. Or combine 1 cup grapes with 1 teaspoon lemon juice, 1 tablespoon honey, and 1 tablespoon brandy; chill thoroughly and serve with sour cream. Good in hot weather.

Seedless Grapes in Sour Cream

Sprinkle grapes liberally with brown sugar and mix with enough sour cream to coat every grape. Chill until ready to use. If brown sugar is too sweet for your taste, use cinnamon sugar and top with a dusting of nutmeg. Serve with crisp cinnamon-sugar cookies.

Baked Peaches

Cut off about an inch of skin from both ends of each peach. Set the peaches—2 for each serving—in a baking dish, sprinkle with lemon juice and sugar, and dot each with ¼ teaspoon butter. Bake in a 350° F. oven about 20 minutes. Serve hot or cold, with or without cream.

Baked Pears

Pare, halve, and core 2 large firm pears or use 4 halves of canned pears. Put in a shallow baking dish with enough water or canned pear juice to cover the bottom. Sprinkle with 1 teaspoon brown sugar, ¼ teaspoon cinnamon, and ⅛ teaspoon ginger on each half, and add ¼ teaspoon butter in each hollow. Bake about 20 minutes in a 350° F. oven. These are good with gingerbread or ginger cookies.

DRIED FRUIT

Dried fruits are apricots, prunes, peaches, and mixed fruit. They are generally bought in 1-pound packages and keep indefinitely if covered. To cook, wash the fruit first and cover with boiling water, 4 cups of water for 1 cup of fruit, and soak for 1 hour. Cook in the same water, with a slice of lemon added, for 30 minutes, simmering over low heat until tender. Add sugar, 1 tablespoon for 1 cup of fruit, about 5 minutes before finished.

Fruit Whip

Use ¾ cup unsweetened fruit pulp—apricots, prunes, or applesauce. Combine with 1 egg white, stiffly beaten, 1 tablespoon sugar, and 1 teaspoon lemon juice. Chill before using and serve with whipped cream or custard sauce. This quantity makes 2 servings. Strained baby food, especially prunes, can be used as a time saver.

———————— ❦ ————————

CANNED FRUIT

Canned fruits are good by themselves and easy to use in other ways, as the preparation steps are eliminated. Unless very small cans are available, some ingenuity is needed to use up the fruit in different ways. Applesauce, berries, and peaches are used in the same ways as the fresh fruit. Apricots, cherries, figs, and plums are not versatile and are generally used plain or in combinations. Canned sliced pineapple can be used in salads, broiled with ham, or used in more elaborate desserts such as upside-down cake. Crushed pineapple is good on ice cream. Canned pears are used in salad or baked the same way as fresh pears; one good way of serving them is to fill each hollow with 1 teaspoon raspberry or any red jam, cover with custard sauce, and chill about an hour. Canned freestone peaches combine well with sour cream and toasted slivered almonds. Flavor Bing cherries with rum or brandy, cover with melted currant jelly, chill and serve with sour cream.

Peaches Baked with Marmalade

Arrange 3 halves of canned freestone peaches in a shallow baking dish. Put 1 teaspoon orange marmalade in each half and sprinkle with a little lemon juice. Pour over some juice from the can so that the bottom of the dish is covered. Place under the broiler for about 10 minutes, until thoroughly heated.

Peach Melba

Put a large peach half (freestone) in a sherbet glass. Fill the center with a scoop of vanilla ice cream and top with prepared Melba sauce. Or make your own sauce from frozen raspberries (see p. 140).

Creamy Pears

Chill canned sliced pears and drain off their juice. Sprinkle with chopped crystallized ginger and serve with whipped cream or cottage cheese.

Baked Canned Pears

Use the recipe for peaches baked with marmalade above and use ginger marmalade instead of orange.

Pineapple Pudding

Fold one part each sweetened whipped cream and drained crushed pineapple into two parts cold boiled rice. Chill. Garnish with slivered almonds or walnut halves.

FROZEN FRUIT

A package of frozen fruit makes 3 servings. Thaw and use alone, as a sauce for cake or ice cream, or in shortcake. A delicious quick dessert can be made by pouring 1 tablespoon rum or sherry over a slice of plain cake, cover with mixed frozen fruit, and top with whipped cream.

Mixed fruit desserts can be made in many combinations of canned, frozen, or fresh fruit and are improved by adding 1 tablespoon of liqueur for each serving: Kirsch (cherry-flavored); Cointreau, Curaçao, or Triple Sec (all orange-flavored); or Grand Marnier. To white fruits such as pineapple, grapefruit, and seedless grapes, add green crème de menthe. These liqueurs are expensive in full-size bottles but last indefinitely; half bottles can be had, or even the tiny size.

Florida fresh fruit salad—oranges, grapefruit, and pineapple—comes in jars, refrigerated. Add banana slices when serving.

Mandarin oranges, in cans, are especially good.

SOME VERY SIMPLE DESSERTS

- Cottage cheese: serve with white or brown sugar and plenty of cream.
- Toasted crackers with cream cheese and jam or guava jelly.
- Gingerbread with chocolate sauce and whipped cream.
- Honey pecan bun, bought at the bakery and heated in the oven, with hot cocoa on the side—very good on a cold night.
- Cupcake, cut in half, with chocolate, lemon, or fruit sauce, or a scoop of ice cream.
- Sponge cake, with fruit or jam and whipped cream.
- Canned rice pudding, rich and creamy, topped with preserved (not canned) quinces, peaches, or cherries.
- Chocolate icebox cake: place three or four chocolate wafer cookies on top of each other with whipped cream between each layer and on top. Chill for at least 3 hours.

PREPARED DESSERT MIXES

- Vanilla: follow directions on the box, chill, and serve with cream and 1 teaspoon of currant jelly. Or make a custard (3 tablespoons mix to 1 cup milk) and use with fruit, cake, shortbread, or trifle. Or flavor with almond extract, sherry, or brandy.
- Butterscotch: use plain with cream, or combine with chopped dates and nuts, or crumbled gingersnaps.
- Chocolate: use plain with cream, or add chopped nuts, or make a mocha pudding by using half milk and half strong coffee.
- Tapioca: add a little almond flavoring and serve with raspberry applesauce.
- Combine fruit-flavored gelatins with leftover fruit.
- Custard mix is not as creamy as the recipe on p. 135.

Lemon Pudding

    1 tablespoon butter
    ⅓ cup sugar
    ½ lemon, juice and grated rind
    1 egg, separated
    1 tablespoon sifted flour
    ½ cup milk

Cream the butter and sugar together, add the lemon and egg yolk, and beat thoroughly. Add the flour gradually and then the milk. Beat the egg white stiff and fold in. Turn into a buttered casserole and set this in a pan of hot water. Bake in a 350° F. oven 40 to 45 minutes or until brown on top. This makes 2 servings.

Lemon Meringue Tarts

CRUST: Roll out ½ cup graham cracker crumbs (about 6 crackers) in a plastic bag, then mix with 2 tablespoons sugar, 2 tablespoons soft butter, and a dash of cinnamon. Line a 6-inch pie plate or 2 custard cups with this mixture, patting it down well. Bake 8 minutes in a 375° F. oven. Allow to cool.

FILLING: Use ½ package lemon pie mix combined with 1 egg yolk. Cook according to directions; when cool, pour into the crust.

MERINGUE: Beat 1 egg white very stiff with 2 teaspoons powdered or confectioner's sugar. Pile this on top of the lemon filling and brown a few minutes under the broiler. Be careful not to burn the meringue.

Rice Cream

Whip ¼ cup heavy cream, add 1 teaspoon sugar, stir, and add ½ cup cold cooked rice. Mix thoroughly and top with strawberry jam. Chill at least 1 hour.

Leftover Cake

Very stale devil's food cake or gingerbread can be reduced to crumbs in the blender and moistened with enough milk to make the consistency of a cornstarch pudding. Add 1 tablespoon of vanilla pudding mix to 2 cups of the cake mixture; cook for 10 minutes over low heat, stirring constantly. Chill, and serve with cream. Chopped nuts can be added. Makes 2 generous servings.

Trifle

Break up about 1 cup of plain leftover cake into a glass dish and dot with currant jelly. Sprinkle with 2 tablespoons sherry and cover with 1 cup custard sauce (p. 138) or vanilla custard mix (p. 133). Chill for several hours and serve with whipped cream.

Mock Cheese Cake

Cut plain pound cake into thin slices. Lay flat and cover all layers except the top with sour cream and brown sugar. Chill well and slice vertically.

Shortbread Custard

Spread three or four sweet crackers of the shortbread type with orange marmalade and stack one above the other. Cover with 1 cup custard sauce (p. 138) which has been flavored with 1 table-spoon sherry just before being removed from the stove. Chill 1 hour before serving.

Baked Custard

  1 cup milk
  1 egg, slightly beaten
  1 tablespoon sugar
      pinch of salt
⅛ teaspoon vanilla extract
      dash of nutmeg

Scald the milk. Combine the egg, sugar, and salt. Add the milk slowly, stirring until the sugar is dissolved. Add the vanilla. Put into a custard cup or any deep individual baking dish and set in a pan of hot water nearly level with the top of the cup. Bake in a 350° F. oven 25 to 30 minutes until firm. Sprinkle with nutmeg and chill. A prepared mix for baked custard makes a palatable substitute with less effort.

Wine Jelly

Soak 1 package (1 tablespoon) plain gelatin in ¼ cup cold water. Add ¾ cup boiling water, ½ cup sugar, and ⅛ teaspoon salt, and stir until dissolved. Then add 2 tablespoons orange juice, 1 table-spoon lemon juice, and ½ cup Madeira wine. Stir well and chill until firm.

Fruit Jelly I

Dissolve 1 envelope strawberry Jello as directed on package and add drained orange and grapefruit segments and blueberries.

Fruit Jelly II

Dissolve 1 envelope lime Jello in 1 cup hot water as directed. Add 1 small can pineapple bits and juice, and about ½ cup seedless grapes.

Coffee Jelly

- ½ tablespoon plain gelatin
- 1 tablespoon cold coffee
- 1 cup hot strong coffee
- 2 tablespoons sugar

Dissolve the gelatin in the cold coffee. Add the boiling coffee and sugar. Stir until gelatin is dissolved. Turn into sherbet glasses to jell; keep in a cool place for several hours until ready to serve. This makes 2 servings. Serve with heavy cream.

Coffee Whip

- 6 marshmallows
- ¼ cup strong coffee
- ¼ cup heavy cream
  unsweetened cocoa

Cut the marshmallows in quarters with scissors dipped in cold water. Add the coffee, boiling hot, and stir until the marshmallows are dissolved. When cool, beat the cream until stiff and fold into the coffee mixture. Chill at least 3 hours. This can be made with extra breakfast coffee. Let it cool while eating breakfast, then add cream and put it in the refrigerator to have ready for dinner. Dust a little unsweetened cocoa over the top.

ICE CREAM

Ice cream and sherbet are hardly worth the trouble of making in small amounts, as so many varieties can be bought easily. A pint averages 3 servings but can be kept frozen in even a very small refrigerator. Use your imagination in serving with sauce, fruit, or a spoonful of liqueur.

MOUSSES

A very simple mousse can be made by whipping ½ cup heavy cream and folding in ½ cup crushed berries or fruit and sugar to taste. Freeze 3 to 4 hours in an ice tray with the controls at the coldest temperature.

To make a quick coffee mousse, whip stiff ½ pint heavy cream; add ¼ cup instant coffee and 3 tablespoons sugar. Put in an ice tray or mold and freeze 3 hours. This should not be too solidly frozen.

ICE CREAM COMBINATIONS

- Coffee ice cream with crème de cacao.
- Chocolate ice cream with crème de menthe.
- Strawberry ice cream with Grand Marnier.
- Fresh peach or raspberry ice cream with meringues from the bakery.
- Raspberry sherbet with fresh blueberries and seedless grapes.
- Orange sherbet with mandarin orange slices and any orange-flavored liqueur.

DESSERT SAUCES

Sweet sauces will improve ice cream, vanilla puddings, and left-over cake; and they are very easy to make. The following are some of the more popular kinds.

Custard Sauce

2 egg yolks
1 egg white
2 tablespoons sugar
pinch of salt
1 cup milk
¼ teaspoon vanilla extract

Beat the eggs together with sugar and salt. Scald the milk in the top of a double boiler. Add milk gradually to eggs. Return to top of double boiler. Stir constantly and, as soon as mixture coats the spoon, remove from the heat. When cool add the vanilla. This makes 2 servings.

Custard sauce can also be made from vanilla pudding mix; use 3 tablespoons of mix to 1 cup of milk and heat until thickened.

Hard Sauce

2 tablespoons butter
¼ cup sugar
¼ teaspoon vanilla extract or 1 teaspoon brandy

Cream the butter and sugar together until thoroughly mixed and light, and add flavoring. Serve with apple betty or any fruit pudding.

Chocolate Sauce

½ cup sugar
1 cup boiling water
1 square cooking chocolate, shaved
⅛ teaspoon salt
½ teaspoon vanilla extract

Combine sugar, water, chocolate, and salt and cook until dissolved. Then cook without stirring until it is the consistency of syrup. Cool slightly and add vanilla. Serve hot or cold. This can be kept in the refrigerator for days and reheated when wanted.

Coffee Sauce

2 tablespoons instant coffee
1 tablespoon flour
dash of salt
1 cup light corn syrup
¾ cup light cream
2 tablespoons butter

Combine the coffee, flour, and salt in a saucepan. Gradually add the syrup, stirring constantly, then the cream and butter. Simmer 5 minutes or until thickened, stirring constantly. Cool before using.

Lemon Sauce

1 tablespoon cornstarch
⅓ cup sugar
⅔ cup boiling water
1½ tablespoons butter
2 tablespoons lemon juice
½ teaspoon grated lemon rind
⅛ teaspoon salt

Mix cornstarch and sugar and add water. Boil for 5 minutes. Remove from heat, add other ingredients, and mix well.

Butterscotch Sauce

⅓ cup brown sugar
1 tablespoon flour
⅓ cup boiling water
1 teaspoon cream
1 teaspoon butter
few drops of vanilla extract
pinch of salt

Mix the sugar and flour in a saucepan and add water slowly, stirring constantly. Cook until thickened and simmer about 2 minutes more, still stirring. Remove from the heat and just before serving add the other ingredients and mix well.

Fruit Sauce

Mash ¼ cup berries or any juicy fruit, such as peaches, put in a double boiler, and add 2 tablespoons of sugar, or more if necessary. Keep over the heat until sugar is thoroughly melted and mixed in. Two tablespoons corn syrup may be added to the fruit without heating. An even easier way to make fruit sauce is with a package of frozen fruit—berries or peaches. Allow to thaw and then give it a whirl in the blender. Fruit with seeds, such as raspberries, should be strained after blending.

14

SAUCES

SAUCES are one of the most interesting parts of cooking and can transform very ordinary ingredients into a delicious dish. The fancy sauces are outside the scope of this book, but the ones included are very easy and will do a lot for your meals, especially leftovers. Be experimental—taste as you go and try all kinds of seasonings, alone or in combination.

Basic White or Cream Sauce

THIN—1 tablespoon butter, 1 tablespoon flour, 1 cup milk.
MEDIUM—2 tablespoons butter, 2 tablespoons flour, 1 cup milk.
THICK—3 tablespoons butter, 3 tablespoons flour, 1 cup milk.
Melt the butter over low heat, blend in the flour, and add the milk gradually, stirring until it is all mixed in. Increase the heat and cook until thickened, stirring occasionally. Season to taste.

MODIFICATIONS OF THIN WHITE SAUCE

NEWBURG SAUCE—add 1 tablespoon sherry.
CURRY SAUCE—add 1 teaspoon onion flakes and 1 teaspoon curry powder.
TOMATO SAUCE—add 1 tablespoon tomato paste.
CHEESE SAUCE—add ¼ cup grated or soft-processed cheese.
EGG SAUCE—add chopped hard-boiled egg and a dash of Worcestershire sauce.

Basic Brown Sauce

½ tablespoon butter
½ tablespoon flour
1 cup meat stock or bouillon
  salt and pepper
½ teaspoon Kitchen Bouquet or any gravy aid

Melt the butter and allow the flour to brown in it, stirring constantly. Add stock gradually and cook until thickened. Add salt and pepper to taste and stir in Kitchen Bouquet to darken. When making gravy for meat, pour off most of the fat in the pan in which the meat has been cooked, substitute it for the butter, add the flour, brown, and add water instead of stock.

Never-Fail Hollandaise

1 tablespoon flour
2 tablespoons melted butter
½ cup water
⅛ teaspoon salt
⅛ teaspoon paprika
  pinch of tarragon
1 egg yolk, slightly beaten
1 tablespoon lemon juice

Stir the flour into half of the butter in the top of a 3-cup double boiler. Keep water in lower half boiling. Add the water slowly, stirring constantly until mixture is smooth and thick. Add seasonings. Stir 1 tablespoon of the sauce into the egg yolk in a little bowl, then add this to the remaining sauce. Add lemon juice and remaining butter, and cook 1 minute. Makes about ¾ cup sauce.

Mock Hollandaise

Blend 1 can condensed cream of chicken soup with ¼ cup mayonnaise and 1 tablespoon lemon juice. Heat, but do not boil. Serve over cooked broccoli, carrots, or asparagus. Makes about 1½ cups sauce.

Quick Hollandaise

1 cup sour cream
  juice of 1 lemon
2 egg yolks
  salt and pepper
  paprika

Put all ingredients in a double boiler and make sure that the top half doesn't touch the water in the bottom half. Stir until the sauce thickens.

Rémoulade Sauce

½ cup chopped pickles or relish
2 tablespoons chopped capers
1 tablespoon prepared mustard
1 tablespoon mixed parsley, tarragon, and chervil
2 cups mayonnaise
  dash of lemon juice (optional)

Blend together the pickles or relish, capers, mustard, herbs, and mayonnaise. If the mayonnaise is stiff, thin it with a little lemon juice. The sauce should be the consistency of soft custard, just able to flow from a spoon. The flavor improves if made ahead of time. Makes about 2¼ cups.

Cucumber Sauce for Fish

Wash, peel, and finely cut 2 cucumbers. Refrigerate with 1 teaspoon salt for 2 to 3 hours in a covered jar. Drain off all fluid; add salt, pepper, and paprika. Just before serving mix in 1 cup plain yogurt or sour cream.

Tartar Sauce

Combine ¼ cup mayonnaise, 1 tablespoon pickle relish, and ¼ teaspoon lemon juice; serve with fish or soft-shell crabs.

Cocktail Sauce

      pepper and Tabasco to taste
  1   cup mayonnaise
  1   tablespoon anchovy paste
  1   tablespoon tarragon vinegar
  2   tablespoons catsup

Add pepper and Tabasco to mayonnaise and blend in remaining ingredients. Makes about 1¼ cups. Use with shrimp or crab.

Sauce for Meat Loaf

Let chopped raw mushrooms stand in sour cream for several hours. Then warm slightly just before serving.

Cranberry Sauce

Put through the meat grinder (medium blade) 4 cups (1 pound) fresh cranberries and 2 seeded, quartered, unpeeled oranges. Stir in 2 cups sugar and chill. Traditionally to accompany turkey but tastes just as good with roast or broiled chicken. Will keep a long time refrigerated.

Raisin Sauce

  2   tablespoons brown sugar
  1   teaspoon flour
  ½   teaspoon dry mustard
      salt and pepper
  ¾   cup boiling water
  2   tablespoons vinegar
  2   tablespoons raisins
  1   teaspoon butter

Mix the dry ingredients, add water and vinegar, and simmer slowly for 10 minutes, stirring well. Add raisins, cook 2 minutes, and add butter. Serve hot with ham or tongue.

Mustard Sauce

Add 2 tablespoons prepared mustard to 1 cup hot white sauce
(p. 141). Serve with ham, tongue or corned beef.

SHORTCUT SAUCES
AND GRAVIES

- Canned gravies, tomato sauce, spaghetti sauces.
- Powdered gravies; mix as directed.
- Canned condensed soups, especially cream of mushroom,
  cream of celery, cream of chicken, cream of onion, Cheddar
  cheese, tomato, and cream of shrimp (for fish and seafood
  dishes). Do not dilute; and test for seasoning.

15

BREAD, COOKIES, AND CAKE

A FULL-SIZE LOAF of bread or a layer cake can present a problem to the single housekeeper unless one has a large appetite for such things and a fine disregard of calories. So-called small family-size loaves of bread can be bought, and small loaf cakes are available frozen and at bakeries. Rolls and muffins are still unpackaged at bakeries, so you can buy as few as you want. If you have freezer space and get tired of the loaf of bread you are reluctant to throw out, just freeze it. This works admirably for vacations and means there will be something on hand when you come home.

Even without freezing, unsliced bread keeps fresh longer than sliced, and all bread keeps better in the refrigerator, especially in damp weather. As for cake, you had better restrain that impulse for a four-layer chocolate concoction or save it for a party. Buy a small loaf cake, or cupcakes, or a few cookies. Angel cake, pound cake, sponge cake, applesauce cake, jelly roll, and macaroons will keep longer than the other kinds. Leftover cake can be used in desserts.

Instead of bread try some other things such as Ry-Krisp or graham crackers, spread lightly with butter and toasted under the broiler, also melba toast in several flavors and sesame crackers. Triscuits and rusks are good this way too. Boston brown bread comes in small cans and goes particularly well with baked beans and fish cakes. Some biscuits come ready mixed—just bake and eat—and there are many prepared mixtures to which only water or water and an egg need be added: popovers, corn bread, rolls, muffins. Use half or even a quarter of the package and follow the directions accordingly. (To halve an egg, beat the white and yolk together and use half of the mixture.) Don't forget English muffins, now in different flavors, butter crumpets, and corn and other "toasts" which only have to be put in the toaster. Cake mixes are also available; use half the package. Some brands offer a "loaf size" package that is half the usual quantity.

An opened package of rolls will keep in the refrigerator, although some of the freshness is lost if the rolls are not all used at one time. The same is true of frozen biscuits. Stale rolls, either baked or not, may be freshened by dipping quickly in cold water and then heated; the same system works with French bread.

Frozen waffles and French toast generally come 6 pieces to the package. Simply pop in the toaster and serve with maple syrup, jam, or honey. Untoasted leftovers can be kept in the freezer. A waffle iron is such an unwieldy extra in a small kitchen that the frozen waffles are a real addition to menu possibilities. Frozen pancake mixes can be used as wanted.

Leftover Bread

MELBA TOAST—use very thin slices and cut in half. Arrange in a pan or on a cookie sheet and dry out in a 300° F. oven until light brown, about 15 minutes. Watch it!

CROUTONS—remove crusts and dice the bread. Sauté gently in melted butter or margarine, turning often so that all the grease is absorbed. Can be flavored with grated cheese, minced garlic, or herbs.

SCALLOPED CHEESE—see p. 54.

FRENCH TOAST—see p. 52.

APPLE BETTY—see p. 125.

BLUEBERRY PUDDING—see p. 126.

Baking Powder Biscuits

    1 cup sifted all-purpose flour
    ½ teaspoon salt
    1½ teaspoons baking powder
    2 tablespoons shortening
    ⅓ cup milk

Sift the flour, salt, and baking powder together in a bowl and cut in the shortening. When well mixed, add the milk gradually until a soft dough is formed. Turn out on a lightly floured board, knead gently to form a ball, and roll with a floured rolling pin to ½-inch thickness. Cut with a biscuit cutter and put on a greased baking sheet. Bake in a 450° F. oven for 12 to 15 minutes.

This makes 6 large or 12 small biscuits; half the quantity can be used if desired. This dough is used for shortcakes served with creamed meat, fish, vegetables, or with crushed fruit; cut in a larger size than the little biscuits. It also makes a good crust for small meat, fish, or vegetable pies.

Blueberry Muffins

    1 tablespoon butter
    ⅓ cup sugar
    1 egg, slightly beaten
    ½ teaspoon salt
    1½ teaspoons baking powder
    1¼ cups sifted all-purpose flour
    ¾ cup milk
    ¾ cup blueberries

Cream the butter and sugar and mix in the egg. Sift the salt and baking powder with 1 cup of flour and add this alternately with the milk. Roll the berries in ¼ cup flour and add them last. Fill greased tins half full and bake 25 minutes in a 400° F. oven. This is also a good way to use up leftover berries.

Quick Nut Bread

¼ cup sugar
1 egg
1¼ cups milk
1½ cups chopped walnuts or pecans
3 cups Bisquick
   whole nuts for decoration

Heat oven to 350° F. Mix the sugar, egg, milk, and chopped nuts, then beat in the Bisquick, hard. Pour into greased loaf pan. Arrange nut halves on top. Bake 45 to 50 minutes. Cool before cutting.

Chocolate Chip Cookies

1 cup sifted all-purpose flour
½ teaspoon baking soda
½ teaspoon salt
½ cup butter
¼ cup brown sugar
½ cup white sugar
1 egg, well beaten
½ cup semisweet chocolate bits

Sift flour, baking soda, and salt together. Cream the butter, add the sugars slowly, and beat thoroughly. Add the egg to this, then the dry mixture gradually, and the chocolate pieces last. Drop by teaspoonfuls on a greased baking sheet and bake 10 to 12 minutes in a 375° F. oven.

Brown Sugar Drop Cookies

To 1 egg white beaten stiff add 1 cup light brown sugar, 1 cup finely chopped pecans, and 1 teaspoon vanilla extract. Drop by teaspoonfuls on a well-greased cookie sheet—not too close together, as they will spread. Bake 1 hour in a 200° F. oven. Makes about 24.

Peanut Butter Cookies

    2   cups sifted all-purpose flour
  1½ teaspoons baking powder
    ½ teaspoon salt
    2   tablespoons butter
    ½ cup peanut butter
    1   cup sugar
    1   egg, well beaten
    1   teaspoon vanilla extract
    ⅓ cup milk
    ½ cup chopped peanuts

Sift flour, baking powder, and salt together. Cream the butter with the peanut butter and beat in the sugar, egg, vanilla, and milk. Stir in the dry mixture gradually. Chill thoroughly. Roll out on a floured board to ⅛-inch thickness. Cut, sprinkle with peanuts, and bake on an ungreased sheet for 10 to 12 minutes in a 375° to 400° F. oven. This makes about 3 dozen cookies and can be cut in half.

This is a good way of using up peanut butter that has gone dry in the bottom of the jar.

Icebox Cookies

    2   cups sifted all-purpose flour
    2   teaspoons baking powder
    ⅛ teaspoon salt
    ⅔ cup butter
    ¼ cup brown sugar
    ½ cup white sugar
    1   egg, beaten well
    ½ teaspoon vanilla extract

Mix and sift the flour, baking powder, and salt together. Cream the butter and add the sugars gradually, beating well together. Add the egg and vanilla, then the dry mixture gradually, beating until smooth. Shape into a roll about 1½ inches in diameter, wrap tightly in waxed paper, and chill for several hours. Cut as many cookies as you want, ⅛ inch thick, and bake on an ungreased sheet 10 minutes in a 400° F. oven.

This recipe can be varied by adding ½ cup chopped nuts. The roll of dough can be kept a long time in the freezer and used up gradually, a few cookies at a time.

Shortbread

Mix 2 cups sifted flour with ½ cup light brown sugar. Work in ¾ cup unsalted butter. Roll out to ⅓-inch thickness and cut in small squares. Bake on a greased cookie sheet at 350° F. for 20 to 25 minutes, or until golden brown. Makes 8 to 12 squares.

Brownies

 1 square chocolate
 2 tablespoons shortening
 ⅓ cup sifted all-purpose flour
 ¼ teaspoon baking powder
  pinch of salt
 ½ cup walnuts, coarsely chopped
 1 egg
 ½ cup sugar
 ½ teaspoon vanilla extract

Melt the chocolate and shortening together in the top of a double boiler, stir until smooth, and allow to cool. Sift the flour, baking powder, and salt together. Stir in nuts. Beat the egg slightly, and add the sugar to it; stir in the chocolate mixture slowly. Add the dry ingredients and beat until smooth. Add the vanilla. Turn into a greased baking pan lined with greased waxed paper. Bake the mixture for 30 minutes in a 350° F. oven. It should be soft when finished and will harden as it cools. Cut into squares as soon as it is taken out of the oven, but leave in the pan until cool.

Butterscotch Brownies

¼ cup butter
1 cup dark brown sugar
1 egg
1 teaspoon vanilla extract
½ cup flour
1 teaspoon baking powder
½ teaspoon salt
¾ cup chopped walnuts or pecans

Preheat oven to 350° F. Cream the butter and sugar together, then beat in the egg and vanilla. Sift together the flour, baking powder, and salt. Fold into the sugar mixture. Stir in nuts. Pour into a greased 9-by-9-inch pan and bake about 25 minutes. Cool. Cut into 16 squares.

Walnut Squares

Combine 1 cup brown sugar with 2 eggs. Sift in 3 tablespoons flour, ½ teaspoon baking powder, and ½ teaspoon salt. Add 1 cup coarsely chopped walnuts. Bake in a greased pan at 350° F. until firm and lightly brown. Cut in squares while still warm.

Jam Sponge

3 eggs
1 cup sugar
1 cup sifted all-purpose flour
1 teaspoon baking powder
1 teaspoon vanilla extract
  jam
  confectioner's sugar

Cream the eggs and sugar together in a bowl. Sift in the flour and baking powder and beat lightly for a few minutes until well mixed. Add vanilla. Put in a greased oblong (11 × 7) pan and bake in a 350° F. oven for 20 minutes. Turn out on a platter or cake rack and when cool cut in half. Spread the lower half with soft jam, put the other half on top and dust lightly with confectioner's sugar. This will keep fresh in a tin box for 10 days.

Applesauce Cake

    1½ cups sifted all-purpose flour
     1 teaspoon baking soda
     ¼ teaspoon salt
     1 teaspoon cinnamon
     ¾ teaspoon cloves
     1 cup chopped nuts
     1 cup chopped raisins
     ½ cup chopped dates (optional)
     ¼ cup shortening
     ⅓ cup brown sugar
     1 egg, well beaten
     1 cup thick applesauce

Sift together the flour, soda, salt, cinnamon, and cloves. Mix about 3 tablespoons of this with the nuts and fruits in another bowl. Cream the shortening with the sugar and add the egg. Add the flour mixture alternately with the applesauce. Add fruit and nut mixture last. Bake in a small greased loaf pan for 40 minutes in a 350° F. oven.

Whole Wheat Carrot Cake

Combine 1 cup grated carrots with 2 eggs, ⅔ cup salad oil, 1 cup brown sugar, and 1 cup whole wheat flour. When well mixed add 1 teaspoon cinnamon, ¼ teaspoon soda, and a dash of salt. Bake in a greased loaf pan for 30 to 35 minutes at 350° F.

16

SANDWICHES

SANDWICHES are the easiest, quickest, and most filling form of snacks or light meals, and are just as appetizing indoors in midwinter as they are at any summer picnic. All kinds of leftovers can be used up as fillings, and for someone living alone they are particularly useful as a way of using up bread before it becomes too stale. If you have a job and eat lunch away from home, you might give some serious thought to making your own lunch and taking it with you, if it is at all practicable with your business arrangements and you prefer a small midday meal. Sandwiches are also good at home with soup or salad for a quick and easy meal. For the lunchbox, make ahead and freeze. If taken out of the freezer at breakfast they will be ready to eat by noon.

SANDWICH BREADS

Besides the usual variations of white, whole wheat, and rye breads that are best with meat and vegetable fillings, there are also date, nut, and Boston brown breads, which are good with cream and cottage cheese combinations, and raisin bread, which combines well with peanut butter and sliced tongue as well as with the soft cheeses. Pumpernickel goes with meat and cheese. Protein bread is advisable for calorie counters. Thaw bread from the freezer half an hour before wanted. Pita bread sandwich pockets are not only tasty but very neat for fillings that might spill out from ordinary slices of bread.

SANDWICH SPREADS

To hold the bread together and to keep the filling in place, both halves of bread are usually buttered. The butter itself can be flavored with anchovy paste, chopped olives, or chopped pickles. Mayonnaise can be flavored in the same way, and should always be used with flaked fish or seafood fillings. Cream cheese may be used plain and softened, if desired, with a little cream, or combined with chopped nuts, olives, chives, pimientos, or capers; it will also need some seasoning. Cottage cheese is softer than cream cheese and can be used in the same combinations. A dash of chili sauce or chutney can be added to any of these spreads. "Sandwich spread," which comes in jars, is a good base for meat or vegetable sandwiches.

Flavored Butter

To make flavored butter allow 2 tablespoons butter to soften and add 1 teaspoon chopped chives and ¼ teaspoon dried tarragon; or 1 teaspoon chopped parsley and a dash of lemon juice; or 1 teaspoon anchovy paste and a dash of lemon juice.

SANDWICH FILLINGS

Egg

- Chopped hard-boiled egg with mayonnaise and a dash of curry powder.

- Chopped hard-boiled egg with mayonnaise, anchovy paste, and capers.
- Chopped hard-boiled egg with mayonnaise and watercress.

Cheese

- Swiss, American, or any sharp cheese on rye or whole wheat bread.
- Cream cheese, dried beef, and thin slices of sweet pickles.
- Cottage cheese with grated carrots or green pepper.

Fish

- Salmon, tuna, or crab meat with mayonnaise and chopped celery.
- Sardines with mayonnaise and chopped egg.
- Shrimp with mayonnaise.

Meat

- Any cold cut, especially liverwurst, ham, or tongue.
- Cold meat loaf.
- Prepared spreads, such as deviled ham or chicken or liver paste (Sell's is excellent).
- Chicken livers and bacon, chopped and mixed.
- Chicken salad.

Vegetable

- Tomatoes, cucumbers, lettuce, watercress, separately or in combinations, with mayonnaise.
- Mushroom stems, sautéed and chopped, with anchovy mayonnaise.

Peanut Butter

- With raisins, bacon, currant jelly, or marmalade.

Sweet

- Marmalade and cream cheese.
- Any red jam and cottage cheese.
- Dates and nuts, chopped and mixed with cream mayonnaise (p. 122).

Fillings for Pita Bread

- Chopped bacon, julienne strips of fresh lettuce or spinach, thinly sliced raw mushrooms and red onion rings, all tossed in a mustard French dressing before putting into the pita.
- Diced feta cheese with chopped black olives, chopped anchovy fillets, and sliced cherry tomatoes.
- Egg salad with chervil mayonnaise and thinly sliced seeded cucumber.
- Sliced avocado, scallions, tomato, and watercress.
- Finely shredded homemade cole slaw with meat of your choice.

HOT SANDWICHES

Hot sandwiches are for home consumption, as they must be eaten immediately. For open-face sandwiches, toast one side of the bread, then spread with the filling and heat under the broiler. Make them of cheese and bacon; cheese and bacon and tomato; cheese and sardines and tomato. A toasted cheese sandwich can be made by spreading in the usual way and simply toasting both sides under the broiler; the cheese will melt as the bread toasts.

English muffins are good with hot cheese, bacon, and tomato combinations. Toast the halves lightly and then spread and heat under the broiler.

Cheese Muffins

Split and lightly toast an English muffin. Spread each half with deviled ham and top with a slice of cheese. Broil until the cheese is melted.

Another good combination is Muenster cheese sprinkled with dried dill.

Blue Cheese Sandwich

Toast 1 slice of bread. Spread with butter, cover with a slice of blue cheese, and heat in a moderate oven 5 to 6 minutes. Sprinkle with chopped salted almonds or peanuts.

Corned Beef and Cheese Sandwich

Combine minced cooked corned beef or corned beef hash with a little Dijon mustard and prepared horseradish. Top with a slice of Muenster or Swiss cheese. Place in a hot oven for about 10 minutes, until cheese is melted and golden brown.

Lobster Roll

Toast both halves of a hamburger bun and fill with lobster salad —lobster meat, chopped celery, and mayonnaise. Equally good with crab, tuna, or chicken salads.

DOUBLE DECKERS

- Ham and American cheese slices—tomato and lettuce.
- Swiss cheese slices and bacon—tomato and lettuce.
- Sardines, boned and skinned, with a sprinkling of lemon juice —tomato and lettuce.
- Chicken or turkey, with a little currant jelly—tomato and lettuce.
- Flaked tuna, sliced egg, mayonnaise—tomato, bacon, and lettuce.
- Salmon, chopped stuffed olives—cream cheese, sliced shrimp.
- Corned beef, sliced sweet gherkins—American cheese, tomatoes.
- Chicken, lettuce—crisp bacon, tomatoes.

Use plenty of soft butter or mayonnaise. Rye bread tastes best by itself, but try combining white and whole wheat. Corn-molasses bread will also add variety. Cheese bread, if you can find it, is wonderful with all cold meats.

17

&

ENTERTAINING
SINGLEHANDED

WHETHER YOU LIVE in a spacious house or one-room apartment, if you have any facilities at all for cooking, you can entertain. Your aim, no matter what kind of entertaining you do, should be to strike a happy medium between the unimaginative and the overfussy; that is, to provide the right amount of "party" atmosphere, so that your guests will feel you consider them worthy of a little extra attention, with an air—to them, at least—of easy and relaxed accomplishment. The secret is this: Don't appear to be trying too hard; do all your planning, and as much as possible of the actual work, well ahead of time.

Good food need not be expensive or exotic or even complicated. The trick is knowing how to make the simplest dishes taste best, how to take shortcuts in preparation, how to produce a meal that is better than average and with just enough imagination to impress your guests with the fact that you have gone to some trouble to please them. The menus that follow attempt to use these principles.

WHAT TO BUY AND SERVE

First, your planning. Remember that even with the most punctual guests a meal is seldom served at the exact hour originally designated—one late-comer or one slow cocktail drinker will upset the schedule. So avoid any dish that will spoil if not eaten immediately.

When you have decided on your menu write it *all* down from cocktails to coffee, and list every ingredient that you will use. Then check with your kitchen staples and make a shopping list. This may sound overmeticulous, but it saves time and trouble in the long run, and the written outline will be your work plan right up to the moment of serving the meal. Make a note of the time to start each operation, and be sure to remind yourself about bread and butter, ice water, sugar for the coffee, and so on. After the marketing is done keep the plan in the kitchen and pin it up with a thumbtack or a bit of Scotch tape where you can glance at it. With nothing to remember lurking in the back of your mind, you will enjoy much more your own predinner cocktail with your guests.

Dinner will consist of at least two courses: a main dish with vegetables, and perhaps salad on the side, and a dessert. Three courses are better, and require only a negligible amount of extra effort: you might make the salad a separate course with cheese and crackers, or you can preface the main course with an appetizer or soup. In any case, each course should be such that it can be kept at the proper temperature until ready to be eaten without any worry on your part. If you provide a delicious and satisfying main course, no one is going to want more than a light dessert. For the same reason, do not spoil the company's appetite ahead of time with too many cocktail snacks.

Now, your main course. If you decide on a casserole—and a very wise decision that will be—you may choose a recipe that will include one or more vegetables. If it is made with potatoes, rice, or spaghetti you should have another vegetable on the side, preferably green. If the green vegetable is already in the casserole, the only accompaniment needed may be a tossed salad. With meat or fish there should be two vegetables, and salad is optional.

In any case, avoid a dish that needs close attention at the last minute—you should not have to do anything except *serve* the food after your guests have arrived. And, whatever your choice may be, see to it that, somewhere between five and seven o'clock, there are twenty or thirty precious minutes, while things are cooking, in which you can shower and change.

WHAT TO DO AHEAD OF TIME

Figure out what shopping can be done ahead of time, and what must be left—such as buying fresh vegetables and breads—until the day of the party. Also plan the preparations that can be made the night before. Probably the dessert can be made ahead of time; a stew can be cooked, placed in the refrigerator, and re-heated later; some dishes can be prepared up to a certain point and continued later; cold soups can be made and given plenty of time to chill. With only one pair of hands, and not too much time, you will be glad to get much of your cookery done before party time. Yes, this generally does mean giving up *two* evenings to one party. On the *third* night you will probably be picking up the pieces and eating the leftovers!

It is possible, even with a crowded schedule, to buy and pre-pare everything for your party on the same day, if you choose quick-cooking foods. Also, weekend entertaining is obviously more leisurely than a workday party. In either case a well-orga-nized work plan is still a great help. Pressure cookers, quick-frozen foods, and canned and other semiprepared foods are won-derful time- and energy-savers; keep well informed about pro-ducts of this kind, which are newly appearing all the time, and use them to cut corners wherever possible.

Check your china, glass, linen, and silver the day before the party. Your menu and work plan will remind you of just what will be needed; set them aside, wash china and glass, polish silver, get out your best linen napkins and use them, even if you generally have paper ones for your lone dinner. Set the table, if possible, before you begin to cook, and cover each place with a clean cloth or dish towel until an hour or so before the guests are expected. If it isn't convenient to set the table ahead of time, collect the things in an easily available place, stacked so that they will not have to be recounted.

FINAL TOUCHES

When seating your guests, be sure to place yourself nearest the kitchen, so that your comings and goings—as few as possible, naturally—will be easily accomplished. A cold first course can be put at each place before you actually sit down; hot soup is better served after the guests are seated, and is brought from the kitchen in the bowls or soup plates. If absolutely necessary, the main course can be put on plates in the kitchen, but it is much nicer to serve it at the table; use a second small table or cart to set the dishes on if they crowd the dining table too much. Serve the salad in a glass bowl. Have bread and butter within reach of everyone, also a pitcher of ice water available; salt and pepper are already on the table, of course. Have the wine ready. Dessert can come in on individual plates or be served at the table, depending on what it is.

If you were really careful about your work plan, you would have reminded yourself in writing to start warming plates and heating rolls when the guests arrive; to make ice water for the table when you take out a tray of cubes for the cocktails; to have the coffee measured in its pot and ready to start brewing when you serve the main course. Such planning keeps you from moving around and helps you enjoy yourself while eating, and talking to your friends. And they will enjoy themselves, with a good dinner, a deft and charming host or hostess, and a general atmosphere of relaxation. When guests want to help you clear away the dishes, let them hand you things from the table but keep them out of the kitchen—it may hold only one person at a time anyway. In your quiet and efficient way you will have *rinsed* off each dish as you changed the courses and stacked the plates; now you can quickly put the silver to soak in a bowl of hot suds, and fill the used pots and pans with hot water. Close the kitchen door and forget the whole business until the party is over. Then put on an apron, set your teeth, and do the dirty work that night, or you'll be very sorry next morning. With the preliminary scraping and rinsing all done, it will not take very long, and you will have the satisfying feeling of a good job well done. (Of course, a dishwasher helps!)

ONE SET OF TOOLS

For entertaining up to three guests the equipment in use for one person will almost certainly be adequate. For five or six guests, larger cooking utensils may be needed, which can also be used for cooking in even larger quantities for a buffet meal of ten or twelve. A roasting pan, a quart-size casserole, a large double boiler, a large saucepan, and possibly a larger shallow baking dish should be adequate. A small electric hot tray is a luxury but useful for parties. Larger serving dishes will also be necessary.

In a small kitchen everything must be put away as soon as it has been used, as every inch is precious. It goes without saying that the utensils used in preparation are washed and put away before the guests arrive, so as to leave the kitchen space clear for serving and later for stacking used dishes. Obviously this also saves time in the grand washing up later on.

Four burners are enough for any meal within reason and should present no problem. A two-burner stove calls for some ingenuity and more careful planning. The cook thus limited should invest in a pot in three sections which, for example, will make soup and two vegetables possible on one burner while the meat cooks on the other. A single oven can be a trial especially if too small to hold two casseroles for a large buffet party. The only solution to this is to bake one casserole, take it out, and keep it hot if possible; bake the second one and serve it first, and let the first dish reheat so as to be ready by the time the guests want second helpings. This is an awkward procedure and takes time, but it is not impossible. Obviously two dishes requiring different baking temperatures cannot be managed, even if the oven is capacious enough to hold them. So watch out for this snag when planning the menu. Many ranges with a single oven do not permit broiling and baking at the same time, so if you plan to broil, a baked dish or dessert cannot be included in the same menu.

The small refrigerator presents as much of a problem as the small range. It must be cleared before marketing is done for the party to allow room for larger than usual amounts of provisions. By the time the meat is taken out to be cooked, the salad should be ready in its bowl (except for the dressing) to sit in the refrigerator until ready to serve. Purists think the salad plates should be chilled as well, but this touch is apt to be too much for limited refrigerator space. Jellied or chilled soup should be put in individual bowls an hour or so before dinner and returned to the refrigerator, if only to save a step at the last minute. If a frozen dessert is on the menu, and it has been made ahead of time, it has to be kept in the freezing compartment, probably displacing a valuable tray of ice; the cook will have to decide which is more important, the frozen dessert or some other kind, probably depending on how much ice will be needed for drinks. If you have a separate freezing compartment it should be possible to freeze and store enough ice well in advance and still allow room for the dessert. If wine is to be chilled this can be a further space problem, especially if the bottle cannot be stored upright.

A gelatin dessert is usually cold enough anywhere in the refrigerator and need not be put in the freezing compartment. Quick-frozen foods, also, if used within twenty-four hours after bought, need only be kept well chilled.

The menus suggested depend on boiling and baking, for two simple reasons: neither method requires much watching, thus leaving the cook free to mingle with the arriving guests, and both allow foods to be kept hot without spoiling, thus removing the worry of an inflexible time schedule. Roasts of meat are not included—they generally take too long and the gravy must be made at the last minute. Frying is avoided because it needs careful watching and also tends to cause smoke and to smell. Broiling is a little easier to manage, as it needs only occasional watching, and the same is true of sautéing and simmering, which are done over low heat with very little danger of burning.

SUGGESTED PARTY MENUS

The kind of party you want to give will probably fall into one of these categories: *seated,* at an attractively set table, two to four people, possibly six if space permits, for lunch, dinner, or supper; *sitting,* six to twelve people, served buffet style; and *standing,* a dozen to however many your room will comfortably hold for cocktails, eggnog, or punch. The following menus, which serve four, include some just for the small dinner, and others that can be adapted for lunch, supper, or buffet. Suggestions, rather than menus, are given for a big party. With these as starters you can branch out and discover the delights of new dishes and new combinations.

❧

DINNER MENUS

❧

Cream of Carrot Soup (p. 41)
Curried Fillets of Sole · Green Rice
Endive with French Dressing
Chocolate Whip

The soup can be made ahead of time and reheated. While the fish is in the oven, cook the rice and chop the parsley to go in it—a blender will do this very quickly. The salad requires practically no preparation; allow one stalk of endive per person. The dessert is made in advance.

Curried Fillets of Sole

8 tablespoons butter (¼ pound)
6 fillets of sole or flounder
1 scallion, top and bulb, chopped
  salt and pepper
1 teaspoon curry powder
¾ cup white wine
2 tablespoons flour
½ cup milk
2 tomatoes, peeled and quartered
¼ pound fresh mushrooms, quartered
1 canned pimiento, quartered

Melt 2 tablespoons butter over medium heat. Add fish, scallion, seasonings, and ¼ cup wine. Cook slowly until fish is white, about 10 minutes. Put fish in a baking dish. Make a sauce of 2 tablespoons butter, flour, and milk, using the same pan in which the fish was cooked; add remaining wine, a little at a time, stirring well. Pour the sauce over the fish; put the tomatoes, mushrooms, and pimiento on top. Dot with remaining butter. Bake 20 minutes in a 350° F. oven.

Green Rice

4 cups cooked white rice
3 tablespoons butter
1 cup chopped parsley

Cook rice according to package directions. Melt butter in skillet. Combine with rice and parsley.

Chocolate Whip

½ pound chocolate bits
2½ tablespoons water
2 tablespoons confectioner's sugar
4 eggs, separated
1 teaspoon vanilla extract
2 packages ladyfingers

Melt the chocolate in the water over low heat; add sugar and the egg yolks, one by one, beating well. Add vanilla. Beat the whites stiff and fold into chocolate mixture. Line a mold or glass dish with ladyfingers, pour in the mixture, and chill overnight. Serves 6. Whipped cream can be added when serving.

Cold Cucumber Soup (p. 45)
Ham Steak in Madeira Sauce (p. 86)
Scalloped Potatoes (p. 106)
Creamed Spinach and Mushrooms
· *Minted Fruit · Cookies*

The soup and dessert are cold. The spinach cooks very quickly. Mix the fruit ahead of time and keep cold. A good menu for hot weather.

Creamed Spinach and Mushrooms

2 packages frozen chopped spinach
1 small can mushroom pieces
½ can concentrated cream of mushroom soup
1 package Lipton's onion soup mix (single serving)
  dash of nutmeg

Cook spinach as directed and drain well. Put in double boiler with drained mushroom pieces, cream of mushroom soup and the onion soup mix. Combine well and add nutmeg. Keep hot over simmering water until ready to serve.

Minted Fruit

grapefruit segments
pineapple pieces
seedless grapes, cut in half
green crème de menthe

Combine fruit (fresh, if possible). Add 1 tablespoon crème de menthe for each serving. Serve very cold.

───────────❀───────────

Caviar Madrilène
Beef Stew · Mixed Green Salad (p. 113)
Fruit or Coffee Mousse (p. 137)

─────────·─────────

The stew can be made the day before, as it improves on reheating. Serve with crisp hard rolls and the red wine used in cooking.

Caviar Madrilène

Use 2 cans madrilène which have not been chilled. Stir in a small jar of red caviar, about 4 tablespoons. Chill until jelled. Top each portion with a teaspoon of sour cream when serving.

Beef Stew

     1 tablespoon butter
 1½ pounds chuck steak, cut in pieces
     1 clove garlic, cut in half
6 to 8 small potatoes, peeled but left whole
6 to 8 small white onions, peeled but left whole
     8 carrots, scraped and cut in 2-inch lengths
    ½ cup water
    ½ cup red wine
       salt and pepper
     1 bay leaf
       pinch each of dried thyme, marjoram, and parsley
     1 tablespoon flour

Melt the butter in a pressure cooker and brown the meat in it with the garlic. Add everything else except flour, cover, and cook under pressure 12 minutes after the indicator is at the cooking point. Reduce steam and open cooker according to manufacturer's instructions. Mix flour in ¼ cup more water, stir into gravy, and cook a few minutes until gravy is thickened. Add gravy coloring, if desired.

To make without a pressure cooker, simmer the meat over low heat for 2 to 3 hours; more liquid will be needed. Add the vegetables for the last 30 minutes only.

———————————— ⊗ ————————————

Assorted Hors d'Oeuvres
Beef Stroganoff
New Potatoes (p. 104) · *Peas Bonne Femme (p. 104)*
Ice Cream or Sherbet with Liqueur (p. 137)

The hors d'oeuvres will take up room in the refrigerator, but with no salad and the dessert in a container until ready to use there should be no space problem. The potatoes and peas will cook themselves while the cook concentrates on the beef for a few minutes.

———————————

Assorted Hors d'Oeuvres

Unless you have an hors d'oeuvres tray, arrange attractively on individual plates. Choose 5 or 6 foods—a sardine (skinless and boneless), half a deviled egg, olives, celery hearts, carrot sticks, and marinated vegetables such as small sliced tomatoes, julienne beets, paper-thin sliced cucumbers, tiny whole mushrooms, potato salad.

Beef Stroganoff

1½   pounds fillet of beef
     flour
 3   tablespoons butter
 2   medium onions, chopped
½   pound mushrooms, sliced
1½   teaspoons salt
⅛   teaspoon pepper
½   cup medium sherry
 1   cup water
 1   cup sour cream

Cut the meat in thin strips, dredge with flour and brown quickly in butter. Remove from skillet. Cook onions and mushrooms in skillet until golden, put back the meat and season. Add sherry and water, bring just to a boil. Remove from heat and stir in sour cream. Heat again but do not boil, and serve immediately.

Smoked Salmon
Coq au Vin · *White Rice (p. 63)* · *Lima Beans (p. 97)*
Coffee Sponge

The chicken and coffee sponge should be made the night before, as the chicken improves on reheating. The rice and beans take about the same cooking time. Rice is recommended because the chicken has such wonderful gravy that not a drop should be lost. The French go after it unashamed with bits of bread.

Smoked Salmon

Buy the best quality at a gourmet store, allowing 2 or 3 slices per person. Serve on individual plates with a wedge of lemon and thin slices of pumpernickel spread with sweet butter. Have the peppermill within reach so that freshly ground black pepper can be added.

Coq au Vin

2	small broilers, cut in quarters
	flour
¼	pound butter
4	slices bacon
8 to 10	small white onions, peeled
¼	pound whole fresh mushrooms
1	clove garlic, finely chopped, or ¼ teaspoon instant garlic
	pinch of dried thyme
1	bay leaf
	several sprigs parsley, tied together
	salt and pepper
¼	cup brandy or sherry
1	cup red wine

Dredge chicken in flour and sear in the melted butter in a large heavy pot. Add bacon, onions, mushrooms, garlic, herbs, and seasonings. Stir until well mixed. Pour the brandy or sherry over the chicken and blaze (light with a match). Add wine, cover pot, and simmer 30 minutes or until chicken is very tender. If sauce needs thickening, add little balls of butter rolled in flour, and stir. Remove the parsley before serving.

Coffee Sponge

1	envelope plain gelatin
1¾	cups strong freshly brewed coffee
½	cup milk
⅔	cup sugar

2 eggs, separated
pinch of salt

Soak gelatin in ½ cup cold coffee. Heat remaining coffee with the milk and sugar in a double boiler. Add soaked gelatin and stir until thoroughly dissolved. Add egg yolks, slightly beaten, and beat until mixture thickens. Remove from heat and beat until it begins to cool. Before it is cold, stir in the egg whites, beaten stiff with a pinch of salt. Pour into a glass dish and allow several hours to chill. Serve with plain cream. This dessert never looks as if it were going to turn out right, but it does.

Watercress Soup
Pork Chops in Sour Cream
Noodles Romanoff (p. 60)
Baked Tomatoes, Cucumber and Zucchini
Scalloped Apples

Watercress Soup

1 bunch watercress, stems removed and chopped fine
2 cups chicken bouillon
2 tablespoons butter
2 tablespoons flour
1 cup light cream
  salt and pepper

Let the cress simmer gently in the bouillon for 10 minutes. Melt the butter in another saucepan and blend in the flour. Add the bouillon and cress gradually, stirring constantly. Bring to boiling point, add cream and seasonings. Serve hot.

Pork Chops in Sour Cream

4 loin pork chops
   salt, pepper and rosemary
1 cup red wine
2 tablespoons sour cream

Cut a piece of fat off one chop and render over low heat until enough grease is obtained to coat the skillet. Braise the meat slowly, 10–15 minutes on each side. Transfer to a baking dish, discarding melted fat. Season with salt, pepper and rosemary, pour the wine over and seal under foil. Bake in a 350° F. oven for 20–25 minutes, adding more wine if necessary. When tender, stir the sour cream into the cooking liquid and heat gently for 5 more minutes.

Baked Tomatoes, Cucumber and Zucchini

Wash 3 small zucchini, not bigger than a quarter in diameter, and slice crosswise. Peel a medium-sized cucumber, cut it in half lengthwise, scoop out the seeds and slice crosswise. Put the zucchini and cucumber in a saucepan, cover with water and bring to the boiling point. Drain and put back in the pan with 1 tablespoon butter, salt and pepper. Cover and cook slowly for 15 minutes. Skin 2 large tomatoes by placing them briefly in boiling water; slice and sauté briskly in a little hot olive oil with 1 teaspoon instant garlic. Add salt and pepper. Combine the vegetables in a deep baking dish, a layer of cucumber and zucchini, then a layer of tomatoes. End with tomatoes on top and sprinkle liberally with grated Cheddar cheese. Brown under the broiler.

Scalloped Apples

½ cup vermouth (sweet or dry)
¼ cup water
1 cup granulated or brown sugar
4 thin lemon slices
4 apples, cored and peeled
1 tablespoon butter

Combine vermouth, water, sugar and lemon. Bring to a boil, reduce heat and simmer 5–10 minutes. Arrange apples in baking dish, pour on the hot syrup, dot with butter. Cover and bake in 400° F. oven until apples are tender, 40 to 50 minutes. Cool, but do not chill. Serve in the syrup, with sweet cream, sour cream or vanilla ice cream.

Curried Chicken Soup
Swedish Meat Loaf · *Green Beans and Mushrooms*
Peach Halves

Curried Chicken Soup

Mix 2 cans of cream of chicken soup with 2 cans bouillon. Heat, add 1 8-ounce jar applesauce and 1 heaping teaspoon curry powder. Serve hot or cold but heat first in any case to blend the flavors.

Swedish Meat Loaf

4 slices white bread, crusts cut off
1 onion, finely chopped
4 sprigs parsley, finely chopped
1 egg, slightly beaten
  salt and pepper
1 pound ground beef
2 tablespoons margarine or butter
1 8-ounce can tomato sauce
1 teaspoon oregano

Soak bread in 1 cup water, mash with fork. Mix bread, onion, parsley and egg with meat and seasonings. Put in a loaf pan, dot with margarine and bake 30 minutes in a 350° oven. Pour on tomato sauce, sprinkle with oregano and bake 20 minutes longer.

Green Beans and Mushrooms

3 cups cut green beans
2 tablespoons butter
1 cup sliced mushrooms
½ cup sour cream
  salt and pepper

Cook the beans until almost tender; drain. Melt butter in a skillet, sauté mushrooms until soft. Add sour cream very slowly, stirring constantly. Remove from heat, season, and mix with beans. Re-heat, if necessary, in a double boiler.

Peach Halves

Use canned freestone ("old-fashioned") peaches. Chill well. Fill the centers with sour cream, top with slivered almonds. Put in a 400° oven for 3 minutes to toast almonds; watch carefully! Allow 3 to 4 halves per serving.

Pâté or Chopped Chicken Livers with Homemade Melba Toast (p. 147)
Lamb Chop Casserole · Whipped Broccoli
Orange Compote

Allow plenty of time for the casserole, which should stew in its own juice until very tender. The broccoli will keep hot in a double boiler.

Lamb Chop Casserole

            4 tablespoons butter
       4 to 6 lean lamb chops
          1½ cups potato balls (made with a ball cutter, or use
             canned)
           12 small white onions, peeled
            1 No. 2 can tomatoes, well drained of juice
            1 4 oz. can mushrooms
            1 cup beef bouillon
            1 teaspoon salt
           ½ teaspoon pepper
            1 teaspoon sugar
            1 tablespoon flour
              juice of ½ lemon
            4 tablespoons sherry

Melt 2 tablespoons butter in a heavy skillet and brown the chops
on both sides. Put potatoes (unless you are using canned) and
onions in a saucepan, cover with water, bring to a boil and cook
for 10 minutes. Put a layer of tomatoes in a 2-quart baking dish,
put the chops in next, add drained potatoes, onions and mushrooms. Pour bouillon over all. Top with another layer of
tomatoes, sprinkle with seasonings and dot with butter. Cover
and cook in a 350° F. oven for 2 hours. Drain off the gravy into
a saucepan, thicken with flour that has been made into a paste
with a little cold water, heat and stir; add lemon juice and sherry
and cook 3 minutes. Pour back into casserole and heat for a few
more minutes.

Whipped Broccoli

Put cooked chopped broccoli through the blender. Mix with
heavy white sauce, season with onion juice, salt and pepper, and
heat in a double boiler. It should be the consistency of mashed
potatoes.

Orange Compote

5 California oranges
1 cup water
¾ cup sugar
⅛ teaspoon salt

Cut the rind off 2 oranges and slice rind into very thin strips. Make a syrup of the water, sugar and salt and boil the rind pieces in it for 20 minutes. Skin and remove membrane from the other 3 oranges and slice all 5. Place in serving bowl and pour the syrup and rind over the slices. Chill well. A tablespoon of rum or orange liqueur may be added before serving.

Shrimp Soup
Veal Cutlets Provençal · Baked Eggplant
Zucchini Salad (p. 116)
Rice Cream (p. 134)

The soup can be hot or cold. The eggplant will cook in the oven while the veal simmers on the range, and neither will need much watching. Double the rice recipe, and instead of topping with jam, you might mold and chill the rice mixture in a ring and fill the center with frozen strawberries or raspberries when serving. Allow time for these to thaw.

Shrimp Soup

Add 1 cup light cream to 2 cans of cream of shrimp soup. Season with ¼ cup sherry and plenty of cayenne pepper. The soup is rather bland and can take plenty of seasoning.

Veal Cutlets Provençal

1½   pounds veal cutlet, well pounded
       flour
       olive oil
 ½   pound fresh mushrooms
   2   cloves garlic, finely chopped
   4   tablespoons dry white wine
   4   ripe tomatoes, peeled, diced, and drained
       salt and pepper
   2   tablespoons chopped parsley

Dip the meat in the flour; sauté in about 2 tablespoons olive oil until brown. Add mushrooms, cut in small pieces; let simmer a few minutes. Sprinkle with chopped garlic. Pour in wine and add tomatoes. Season, cover, and let simmer 10 to 15 minutes. Sprinkle with parsley when ready to serve.

Baked Eggplant

   1   large eggplant
       butter
   4   small onions, minced
   4   tablespoons minced green pepper
   4   tomatoes, sliced
       salt and pepper
       bread crumbs
       grated cheese

Peel and cut eggplant into 1-inch cubes. Cook 15 minutes, covered, in boiling salted water. Drain well. While this is cooking, sauté in butter the onions and green pepper; cook until soft over low heat. Combine with the eggplant and tomatoes. Season with salt and pepper. Put in a greased casserole, top with bread crumbs and grated cheese, and dot with butter. Bake 30 minutes in a 400° F. oven, until the cheese is melted and the top is brown.

Consommé
Chicken in Red Wine
Zucchini and Rice Casserole
Orange Cream

Use a good canned consommé (not bouillon) and lace liberally with sherry. If serving hot, top with a thin slice of lemon; if jellied, serve with a lemon wedge. The main course cooks itself. A green salad could be added if desired. Make the dessert ahead of time.

Chicken in Red Wine

1 chicken cut into serving pieces, or 2 whole breasts cut in half
   salt and pepper
½ cup butter, softened
½ teaspoon tarragon
¼ teaspoon basil
1 tablespoon chopped parsley
1 tablespoon finely chopped scallions or instant onion
   dry red wine

Preheat the oven to 375° F. Place the chicken in a shallow baking dish. Mix together the butter and herbs and smear over the top of the chicken. Pour wine down the side of the dish until it comes halfway up the chicken. Bake uncovered 40 minutes or until browned and tender.

Zucchini and Rice Casserole

 2 medium zucchini, cut crosswise into ¼-inch-
       thick slices
⅓ cup shredded Cheddar cheese
⅓ cup raw rice
 1 can condensed cream of mushroom soup
      salt and pepper

In a well-buttered casserole, layer the zucchini, cheese and rice, repeating twice. In a saucepan, combine the soup with seasonings and an equal amount of water and heat. (Some canned sliced mushrooms could be added if desired.) Pour most of this over the zucchini. Bake, covered, 25 minutes, then uncover and bake another 20 minutes, at 375° F. Add more of the heated sauce if casserole seems dry. Give this dish a 5-minute head start on the chicken.

Orange Cream

 1 package orange-flavored gelatin
 1 cup hot water
 1 8-ounce cream cheese, quartered
½ cup orange juice
 2 tablespoons lemon juice
 1 strip orange rind

Blend the gelatin and water on high speed for 10 seconds. Add the remaining ingredients, cover and blend on high speed for 20 seconds. Pour into 3 or 4 individual molds and chill until firm. Unmold and serve with raspberry sauce (p. 140).

———————————— ✿ ————————————

LUNCHES, SUPPERS, OR LIGHT DINNERS

The next five menus, which also serve four, could be used for dinner but would be equally appropriate for lunch or supper. For a lighter meal you might skip the first course and serve only fruit or cheese and crackers for dessert.

———————————————

Cold Stuffed Tomatoes
Veal Paprika (p. 87) · *Fresh Asparagus (p. 96)* ·
Noodles
Strawberries, Blueberries, and Mandarin Oranges
Flavored with Cointreau

Double the recipe for the veal; it needs attention only at the last minute. When the noodles are cooked, drain and mix thoroughly with butter; keep hot in a double boiler.

———— · ————

Cold Stuffed Tomatoes

Choose small and very ripe tomatoes. Plunge into boiling water, remove, peel, and chill thoroughly. Scoop out center and fill with crab meat or lobster salad, chicken or egg salad, or red caviar with sour cream. One stuffed tomato makes one serving.

———— · ————

———————————— ❧ ————————————

Mulligatawny Soup
Shrimp Aspic · Celery and Potato Salad
Angel Cake with Cocoa Cream

Appropriate for hot weather. The soup should be filling and hot, the salad delicate and cold. If the aspic is made in a ring, fill the center with the salad. The dessert must be made ahead of time.

Mulligatawny Soup

1 can condensed cream of chicken soup
1 can condensed cream of mushroom soup
1 cup chicken stock
1 cup light cream
1 teaspoon curry powder

Combine thoroughly and heat in a double boiler.

Shrimp Aspic

2 envelopes plain gelatin
1½ cups cold chicken broth
½ cup boiling chicken broth
3 tablespoons lemon juice
⅔ cup dry white wine
   salt and paprika
2 cups cooked or canned shrimp, cleaned and drained
4 hard-cooked eggs, sliced
1 cup sliced cucumber
1 green pepper, cut in rings

Soak the gelatin in ½ cup cold broth; add ½ cup hot broth to dissolve. Add remaining broth, lemon juice, wine, and seasonings. Chill. When it starts to set, add shrimp, eggs, cucumber, and green pepper. Pour into a mold and chill for several hours.

Celery and Potato Salad

For each serving, dice a cold boiled potato, add 1 heaping table-spoon finely chopped celery and 1 chopped scallion. Mix, season with salt and cayenne or paprika, a dash of dill weed or savory, then mix thoroughly with mayonnaise. Chill. Serve with lettuce if desired.

Angel Cake with Cocoa Cream

7	teaspoons unsweetened cocoa
7	teaspoons sugar
1	pint heavy cream
¼	teaspoon vanilla extract
8- to 9-inch	ready-made angel cake

Mix cocoa, sugar, and cream, and chill well. Then whip and add vanilla. Cut off the top of the cake ring, scoop out a little of the middle to form a shell, and fill with the cream mixture. Put the top back and frost the whole cake with the remaining cream. Chill several hours.

Broccoli Soup
Risotto of Chicken Livers and Mushrooms
Vegetable Salad (p. 113)
Apricot Icebox Cake

The salad ingredients and the dessert are prepared ahead of time. The risotto can simmer away without much attention until the bouillon is absorbed, then watch it and serve without delay.

Broccoli Soup

Dilute 2 cans cream of chicken soup according to directions; add 1 cup cooked broccoli and mix in the blender until smooth.

Risotto of Chicken Livers and Mushrooms

  ¼ pound butter
   4 small onions, peeled and minced
1½ cups uncooked white rice
    salt and pepper
   4 cups chicken bouillon
   1 pound fresh mushroom caps
   1 package frozen chicken livers
    grated Parmesan cheese

Melt 6 tablespoons of the butter in a large heavy skillet; brown the onions lightly in it. Add rice and fry 10 minutes, stirring to prevent sticking. Season, add half the bouillon, and simmer, covered, 15 minutes. Add the remaining bouillon; simmer for another 15 minutes. All of the liquid will be absorbed, and the rice should be tender. While this is cooking, sauté the mushroom caps and chicken livers in another pan, in 2 tablespoons butter. Combine with rice. Stir, heat, and serve sprinkled liberally with cheese.

Apricot Icebox Cake

    2 packages ladyfingers
1 to 2 cups apricot jam
    1 package (3¼ oz.) vanilla pudding mix
  2½ cups milk
    whipped cream

Line a 6 × 10-inch glass dish with the ladyfinger halves and spread as thickly as desired with the jam. Cook the pudding as directed but with a little more milk than specified. When cooked, pour over the cake and jam, and allow about 2 hours to cool. Cover with whipped cream before serving.

Melon Balls
Chicken Tetrazzini · Spinach and Artichokes
Gingerbread with Chocolate Sauce

Make the chicken dish first and let it bubble gently
in the oven at the temperature required for baking
the gingerbread—use a mix for this. The chocolate
sauce (p. 139) will keep hot in a double boiler until
wanted.

Melon Balls

Choose any good ripe melon but one that is still firm and not
mushy. Cut in half, remove the seeds and pulp. With a ball cutter
scoop out the fruit and serve in sherbet glasses, about 8 balls per
serving. Top with a little fresh chopped mint.

Chicken Tetrazzini

¼ cup butter or margarine
¼ pound mushrooms or 4-ounce can
¼ cup flour
½ teaspoon salt
⅛ teaspoon pepper
1½ cups milk
½ cup chicken stock or bouillon
2 cups diced cooked or canned chicken
½ 8-ounce package thin spaghetti, cooked
grated Parmesan cheese

Melt the butter; sauté mushrooms 3 minutes over low heat. Stir
in the flour and seasonings; add milk and stock or bouillon gradu-

ally, stirring until the mixture thickens. Add chicken and cooked spaghetti, well drained. Place in a baking dish. Cover thickly with cheese and bake in a 375° F. oven 20 minutes.

Spinach and Artichokes

Line a casserole with 1 can artichoke hearts, drained. Cook 2 packages frozen creamed spinach according to directions on the package. Pour over the artichokes. Make a sauce of 1 cup sour cream, 1 cup mayonnaise and ¼ cup lemon juice. Pour it over the spinach. Top with enough mushroom caps to cover. Bake 20 minutes in a 350° F. oven.

Tuna à la King (p. 74)
Rice · Artichokes Hollandaise (pp. 96 and 142)
Rum Charlotte

Double the tuna recipe. Serve the artichokes on separate plates with plenty of sauce—or melted butter, if you prefer. Soup is optional with this meal.

Rum Charlotte

Line a glass dish with ladyfingers that have been dipped very quickly in light cream. Fill the middle of the dish with whipped cream, sweetened and flavored with rum. Top generously with grated bitter chocolate and chill thoroughly.

MENUS FOR BUFFET

Seafood Newburg · Green Rice Ring
Lettuce, Endive and Watercress Salad
Strawberries in Shells

Seafood Newburg

1　8-ounce can each tuna, shrimp and crab meat
2　tablespoons butter
2　tablespoons flour
2　cups whole milk
　　salt and pepper
¼　cup medium sherry

Wash and drain the shrimp. Drain and separate the crab meat. Drain and flake the tuna. Melt the butter, stir in the flour and, when well mixed, add milk gradually, stirring continually. Add seasonings. When sauce is thick, add sherry. Combine with tuna, shrimp and crab meat in a baking dish. Bake 20–25 minutes in a 350° F. oven. 4 servings.

Green Rice Ring

Combine 4 cups cooked white rice with 1 cup minced parsley and 3 tablespoons minced onions that have been cooked until soft in ⅓ cup melted butter. Pack into a greased ring mold, and let stand a few minutes in a hot oven. Unmold on a large plate and fill the center with the Newburg. 4 generous servings.

Strawberries in Shells

Moisten the inside of sponge cake shells with sherry. Thaw frozen strawberries and heap in the shells. Top with sour cream. Fresh berries could be used but the frozen have more juice.

Cold Cuts—Turkey, Roast Beef, Ham, Tongue
Cauliflower au Gratin
Salad of Greens, Tomatoes, Cooked Green Beans, and
Chopped Hard-Cooked Eggs
Fruit Tarts or Éclairs

This is almost too easy. Get the meats from the delicatessen and the dessert from the bakery. Prepare the salad while the cauliflower is cooking. This menu can be expanded to feed any number served buffet style.

Cauliflower au Gratin

One head will serve 4 to 6. Cook according to directions on p. 100. Allow to cool. Separate into small pieces. Put in a greased casserole with cheese sauce (p. 141) or Cheddar cheese soup. Sprinkle the top liberally with grated cheese. Bake in a 350° F. oven until the cheese is melted and starting to brown, about 15 to 20 minutes.

Kidney Stew
Mixed Vegetable Salad
Pineapple Bavarian

Kidney Stew

      8 lamb kidneys
        salt and pepper
      ½ pound sliced fresh mushrooms
      1 bunch scallions, chopped (6 or 8)
      4 tablespoons butter
      3 tablespoons flour
      ½ cup bouillon
      ½ cup dry red wine
   1½ cups potato balls, cooked or canned

Split the kidneys and soak in salted water for 30 minutes; rinse, slice—removing membranes—and season. Sauté with mushrooms and scallions in the butter for 10 minutes, then put in baking dish. Add the flour to the butter remaining in the skillet, mix well. Add the bouillon and wine gradually to make a gravy; stir and cook until thickened. Add to kidneys. Add potatoes, cover and simmer in a 350° F. oven for 25 minutes. 4–6 servings.

Mixed Vegetable Salad

Tear Boston or romaine lettuce into bite-sized pieces. Add thinly sliced radishes, zucchini and scallions, finely chopped celery and green peppers, and cherry tomatoes, cut in half. Mix with French dressing.

Pineapple Bavarian

1   tablespoon plain gelatin
¼   cup cold water
½   cup sugar
2   tablespoons fresh lemon juice
1   cup crushed canned pineapple
1   cup heavy cream

Soak gelatin in water for 5 minutes, then cook in a double boiler with the sugar, stirring until dissolved. Add lemon juice and pineapple and let cool until mixture is syrupy. Whip cream until stiff and fold into gelatin mixture. Turn into a mold or glass dish and chill 3–4 hours. 4–6 servings.

Curried Chicken
Boiled White Rice · Tossed Green Salad (p. 113)
Layer Cake

Follow the basic recipe for curry on p. 92, multiplying the quantities to suit your needs—a whole, 3-pound chicken, when cooked and the meat taken off the bones, should serve 5 or 6. Keep hot in a double boiler until ready to serve. Put the rice in a colander over gently steaming water. See page 92 for suggested accompaniments to curried dishes. For dessert you might serve the best cake you can buy—or make.

Cold Salmon
Vegetable Platter
Key Lime Pie

Allow 3 servings per pound of fish. Cook according to directions on p. 70 and chill for several hours. Peel off and discard the skin, but leave the fish in one piece on the bones. Serve a big bowl of rémoulade sauce (p. 143) and a dish of finely sliced cucumbers in French dressing. Pass hot buttered rolls, if desired.

Vegetable Platter

Arrange on lettuce around the salmon, if there is room, or on a separate platter, chilled sliced tomatoes, sliced hard-boiled eggs, fresh cooked asparagus, or whole green beans. The rémoulade sauce seasons these as well as the fish.

Key Lime Pie

13 graham crackers, finely crushed
4 tablespoons butter, melted
3 egg yolks
1 can condensed milk
¾ cup fresh lime juice
  whipped cream

Make a pie crust by combining graham crackers and butter. Line a pie plate with this mixture. For the filling, beat the egg yolks lightly, add the condensed milk, and beat again. Add the lime juice and beat until smooth. Pour into the pie shell and chill. Just before serving, top with whipped cream (the ready kind in a pressurized can will do very well).

COCKTAIL PARTY SUGGESTIONS

Finally, the big party. What liquor you serve depends on your choice. It is useful to know, when calculating what to buy, that a full quart of spirits yields 21 portions, a fifth 17; a bottle of wine 6, and fortified wine—sherry—12. Remember two rules about drinks: keep them simple, and serve them cold. It will probably be necessary to supplement your own ice trays by buying extra cubes. If space is a problem, set the container in the bathtub and refill the ice bucket as necessary.

As to accompanying foods, three warnings: dips drip, and "dippers" are apt to crumble; hot canapés cool rapidly and lose their appeal; salty foods create thirst. In addition to the usual nuts, olives (green and ripe), tiny sweet pickled gherkins, cherry tomatoes, and whatever, you might consider the following:

Stuffed Raw Mushrooms

Choose large caps and snap off the stems. Fill with seafood or chicken salad, or cream cheese mixed with chives and horseradish.

Marinated Mushrooms

Buy small whole button mushrooms in cans (not the kind in butter). Drain off the juice. Put mushrooms in a bowl or jar with 1 small white onion minced fine and a bay leaf broken into small pieces, for each can. Cover with olive oil and refrigerate at least overnight. They will keep a long time if tightly covered. Serve on toothpicks.

Cheese Board

Arrange on a cheese board three types of cheese and provide a sturdy knife for each. Soft cheeses might include Liederkranz or Danish cream cheese; firm ones, Bel Paese or Bonbel; hard ones, Edam or a good sharp Cheddar. Have melba rounds—the sesame seed ones are particularly good—or Triscuits rather than the more crumbly salted crackers.

Deviled Eggs

See p. 48 for basic directions. Vary the yolk filling by adding a little deviled ham to some, curry powder or herbs to others. Allow two halves per guest. These can be made well in advance. Cover with Saran Wrap and refrigerate.

Tomato Canapés

Recommended because they don't cool off or get soggy. Choose small firm ripe tomatoes and slice with a very sharp knife. Cut rounds of white bread just larger than the tomatoes and spread with mayonnaise in which a pinch of basil has been allowed to stand a few hours. Put the tomato slices on top and sprinkle with salt and a little white pepper.

Chopped Chicken Livers

Put cooked chicken livers through the meat grinder, mix with mayonnaise, season with onion salt and powdered marjoram. Chill well before using. Serve with melba toast rounds or crackers.

Cucumber Canapés

Peel a cucumber and slice not too thin, about ⅝ inch. Mix softened cream cheese with horseradish, celery seed and onion salt. Spread on the cucumber slices and dust with paprika. Keep well chilled until ready to serve. This is particularly good in hot weather when other canapés might wilt.

Almond Cheese Canapés

Cover rounds or strips of hot buttered toast with a generous amount of Roquefort cheese. Dust with cayenne pepper and heat in a moderate oven for 5 minutes. Add chopped salted almonds and serve immediately.

Clam Puffs

Combine canned minced clams (well drained) with cream cheese and a dash of horseradish. Spread on toast rounds and broil briefly until the cheese starts to puff up.

Raw Vegetables or Shrimp

Serve with a bowl of mayonnaise flavored with onion salt and curry powder. Vegetables might include carrot sticks, cherry tomatoes, strips of green and red peppers, celery hearts, cucumber sticks, spring onions, cauliflowerets. While this is a dip and you'd better have a supply of paper napkins on hand, vegetables and shrimp do not collapse like potato chips.

Bologna Sandwich

Take 4 or 5 slices of bologna sausage and spread each slice with softened cream cheese and a little horseradish. Stack the slices in sandwich fashion. Chill for several hours. To serve, cut in 6 to 8 pie wedges.

Bacon Crisps

Mince raw bacon into tiny squares and fry until light brown. Dry on paper towel. Spread rounds—toast, melba toast, or crackers—with chunky peanut butter; sprinkle the bacon on top. These should not be refrigerated or made too long in advance, as the bacon will get soggy.

INDEX

· NOTES ·

· NOTES ·